SUMMER SKILLS 5

For the Child Going into FIFTH GRADE

Written by **SHANNON KEELEY**

Illustrations by **JUDY STEAD**

Cover illustration by Amy Vangsgard

Flash Kids
A Division of Barnes & Noble
122 Fifth Avenue
New York, NY 10011

ISBN: 978-1-4114-0348-2

Please submit all inquiries to FlashKids@bn.com

Printed and bound in China

7 9 11 13 15 14 12 10 8

DEAR PARENT,

Your child is out of school for the summer, but this doesn't mean that learning has to stop! In fact, reinforcing academic skills in the summer months will help your child succeed during the next school year. This Summer Skills workbook provides activities to keep your child engaged in all the subject areas—Language Arts, Math, Social Studies, and Science—during the summer months. The activities increase in difficulty as the book progresses by reviewing what your child learned in fourth grade and then introducing skills for fifth grade. This will help build your child's confidence and help him or her get excited for the new school year!

As you and your child go through the book, look for "Fast Fact" or "On Your Own" features that build upon the theme or activity on each page. At the back of this book you'll find a comprehensive reading list. Keep your child interested in reading by providing some or all of the books on the list for your child to read. You will also find a list of suggested summer projects at the back of this book. These are fun activities for you and your child to complete together. Use all of these special features to continue exploring and learning about different concepts all summer long!

As your child completes the activities in this book, shower him or her with encouragement and praise. You can feel good knowing that you are taking an active and important role in your child's education. Helping your child complete the activities in this book provides him or her with an excellent example—that you value learning, every day! Have a wonderful summer, and most of all, have fun learning together!

TABLE OF CONTENTS

FISHING AROUND

Find the sentence that has the same meaning as the underlined word. The first one is done for you.

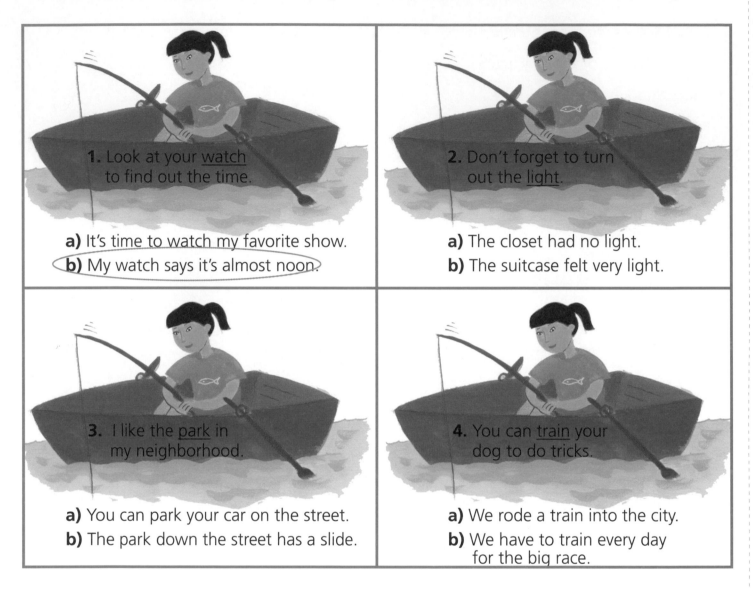

1. Look at your <u>watch</u> to find out the time.

a) It's time to watch my favorite show.
b) My watch says it's almost noon.

2. Don't forget to turn out the <u>light</u>.

a) The closet had no light.
b) The suitcase felt very light.

3. I like the <u>park</u> in my neighborhood.

a) You can park your car on the street.
b) The park down the street has a slide.

4. You can <u>train</u> your dog to do tricks.

a) We rode a train into the city.
b) We have to train every day for the big race.

Each word in the can has two meanings.
Pick a word from the can and write a sentence for each meaning.

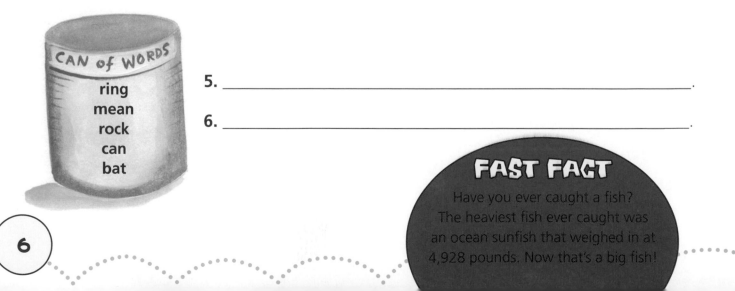

CAN of WORDS

ring
mean
rock
can
bat

5. _____.

6. _____.

FAST FACT

Have you ever caught a fish?
The heaviest fish ever caught was
an ocean sunfish that weighed in at
4,928 pounds. Now that's a big fish!

RALPH'S ROTTEN DAY

Read the story and fill in the chart to show the cause and effect.

It all started when Ralph's alarm clock didn't go off in the morning. He woke up late and didn't have time for breakfast. Ralph ran out the door, and he kept running all the way to school. In fact, he ran so fast that he tripped and fell down! Ralph made it to school just as the bell rang.

Ralph's teacher, Mr. Grundy, asked the students to hand in their homework. Ralph had forgotten his homework, so he was the last person to be dismissed for lunch. "At least I didn't forget my lunch," Ralph thought.

At lunchtime, Ralph sat at the lunch tables with his friends and ate his sandwich. Maybe his rotten day was over. As he stood up from the table, he noticed something sticky on his pants. Ralph had sat on bubble gum! For the rest of the day, every time Ralph sat down, he stuck to the chair.

"Let's hope your rotten luck doesn't stick around much longer!" Mr. Grundy joked.

Cause	Effect
The alarm clock didn't go off.	1. Ralph woke up late and didn't have time for breakfast.
Ralph ran to school very fast.	2.
3.	Ralph was the last person dismissed for lunch.
4.	Every time Ralph sat down, he stuck to the chair.

ON YOUR OWN

Imagine what would happen if you overslept! Make a list of all the things that might happen if you didn't wake up on time.

7

SUNNY SUMS

Add or subtract the numbers.

1. 3452
  − 1435
    2017

2. 3177
  + 2354

3. 5041
  − 3405

4. 1989
  + 4036

5. 7432
  − 5219

6. 4820
  + 2129

7. 6271
  − 2480

8. 2364
  + 3478

9. 8710
  − 1842

10. 4836
  + 3719

11. 4321
   3210
  + 356

12. 2645
   1082
  + 226

13. 1573
   1827
  + 4451

14. 3509
   4055
  + 1021

FAST FACT

Most of the time ocean water is blue because it reflects the color of the sky. The Red Sea, however, looks red because of the red algae living in the water. The Black Sea looks black because the water has a black substance called hydrogen sulfide in it.

BEACH BLANKET BLAST

Fill in the blanks to complete the number families on the beach blanket. Watch the signs!

1. 4, 3, 12

$\underline{4} \times \underline{3} = \underline{12}$

$\underline{3} \times \underline{4} = \underline{12}$

$\underline{12} \div \underline{4} = \underline{3}$

$\underline{12} \div \underline{3} = \underline{4}$

2. 6, 4, 10

$\underline{6} + \underline{4} = \underline{}$

$\underline{} + \underline{} = \underline{}$

$\underline{} - \underline{} = \underline{}$

$\underline{} - \underline{} = \underline{}$

3. 5, 6, 30

$\underline{5} \times \underline{6} = \underline{}$

$\underline{} \times \underline{} = \underline{}$

$\underline{} \div \underline{} = \underline{}$

$\underline{} \div \underline{} = \underline{}$

4. 7, 3, 21

$\underline{7} \times \underline{3} = \underline{}$

$\underline{} \times \underline{} = \underline{}$

$\underline{} \div \underline{} = \underline{}$

$\underline{} \div \underline{} = \underline{}$

5. 8, 6, 14

$\underline{8} + \underline{6} = \underline{}$

$\underline{} + \underline{} = \underline{}$

$\underline{} - \underline{} = \underline{}$

$\underline{} - \underline{} = \underline{}$

6. 5, 4, 20

$\underline{5} \times \underline{4} = \underline{}$

$\underline{} \times \underline{} = \underline{}$

$\underline{} \div \underline{} = \underline{}$

$\underline{} \div \underline{} = \underline{}$

7. 9, 8, 72

$\underline{9} \times \underline{8} = \underline{}$

$\underline{} \times \underline{} = \underline{}$

$\underline{} \div \underline{} = \underline{}$

$\underline{} \div \underline{} = \underline{}$

8. 5, 6, 11

$\underline{5} + \underline{6} = \underline{}$

$\underline{} + \underline{} = \underline{}$

$\underline{} - \underline{} = \underline{}$

$\underline{} - \underline{} = \underline{}$

9. 8, 7, 56

$\underline{8} \times \underline{7} = \underline{}$

$\underline{} \times \underline{} = \underline{}$

$\underline{} \div \underline{} = \underline{}$

$\underline{} \div \underline{} = \underline{}$

ON YOUR OWN

You don't have to go to the beach to make a sand castle. Just find a sandy spot, and use some water to moisten the sand. Use buckets and shovels to make shapes and build your own castle.

WHO'S THE BOSS?

Read about the three levels of government.
Then write some notes in the space below about what each level does.

No matter where you live in the United States, you have three groups of leaders looking out for you. Your **local** neighborhood is part of a city or town. People in your town elect a mayor as a leader. Each city has a school district to oversee the schools in its area. Cities and towns are grouped into a larger area, called a county. Your city or county provides police officers and firemen to protect the people.

You are also a citizen of the **state** where you live. The governor is the head of a state and has lots of people to help him or her. In fact, each state has three branches of government: executive, legislative, and judicial. Each state also has its own constitution. State governments can give out licenses, like a driver's license. They have to oversee businesses within the state as well.

All the states belong to the **federal** government. The federal government also has executive, legislative, and judicial branches of government. These three branches are explained in the U.S. Constitution. The federal government has a lot of responsibilities. It prints money and oversees the post office. It also provides armed forces to protect our country. Only the federal government can declare war or make a treaty with another country. The president is the head of the executive branch.

Whether it's local, state, or federal government, they all have the same main purpose. They look out for the well-being of the citizens!

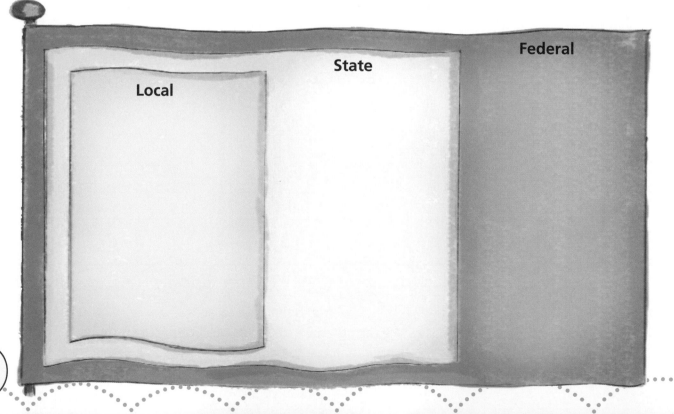

Federal

State

Local

IT'S A JUNGLE OUT THERE!

List some of the food chains that are part of this web.

Leopard

Lion

Zebra

Giraffe

Baboon

Acacia Tree

Grasses

1. <u>Acacia Tree</u>   <u>Giraffe</u>   <u>Lion</u>
2. _____   _____   _____
3. _____   _____   _____

For each pair of animals, figure out which one is the predator and which is the prey. Label each animal.

4. Leopard   Baboon   **5.** Giraffe   Lion
_____   _____   _____   _____

6. Lion   Zebra
_____   _____

Use the food web to complete the lists.

7. Herbivores, or animals that eat plants: **8. Carnivores**, or animals that eat meat:
_____   _____
_____   _____
_____

ON YOUR OWN

Make a list of the animals that live
in your own backyard or neighborhood.
Then divide the list into herbivores
and carnivores.

RAINING CATS AND DOGS

Have you ever heard the expression "It's raining cats and dogs"? This is an example of an **idiom**. The expression means something different from what the words usually mean. This phrase just means that it's raining very hard, not that cats and dogs are falling from the sky!

Draw a line to match each idiom with its meaning.

1. Once in a blue moon	**a)** through good times and bad times
2. Hit the nail on the head	**b)** to give away a secret or surprise
3. Learn the ropes	**c)** once in a while
4. Stick out your neck	**d)** very easy
5. A piece of cake	**e)** to learn the basics
6. On cloud nine	**f)** to get something exactly right
7. Through thick and thin	**g)** to go out of your way or take a risk
8. Let the cat out of the bag	**h)** very happy

FAST FACT

How did the idiom "It's raining cats and dogs" start? Here's one explanation: In Northern Europe, cats were a symbol of rain and dogs were a symbol of wind. So, when a rainstorm hit, people said "It's cats and dogs out there!"

THE GEBETA BOARD: AN ETHIOPIAN FOLKTALE

A man carved a beautiful game board, called a gebeta board, out of wood and gave it to his son. The boy loved playing games with the gebeta board and took it everywhere with him.

One day, he came upon a group of men who had no wood to start a fire. The boy gave them his gebeta board to use for firewood. The gebeta board went up in flames, so the men gave him a new knife in its place.

Next, the boy came upon a man digging a well. The boy gave him his new knife to dig with. The ground was so hard that the knife broke. So, the man gave the boy a new spear to take its place.

The boy continued on and met a group of hunters. The hunters used the boy's spear to kill a lion. The spear cracked, so the hunters gave the boy a new horse in its place.

The boy and horse met a group of men working on the road. The workmen made so much noise, the horse got frightened and ran away. The workmen gave the boy an ax in place of the horse.

The boy took the ax and walked toward his village. He lent his new ax to a woodcutter. The woodcutter broke the ax, but he gave the boy a limb of the tree.

The boy carried the limb back to the village. He gave the tree limb to a woman who needed wood for her fire. As the wood went up in flames, the boy began to cry. So, the woman gave him a gebeta board in its place.

When the boy got home, his father smiled and said, "What is better than a gebeta board to keep a boy out of trouble?"

A group of men used the board for firewood and gave the boy a _____knife_____ in its place.
                                                                   1.
When the knife broke, a man gave the boy a _____ in its place.
                                              2.
When the _____ broke, the hunters gave the boy a _____ in its place.
           3.   **4.**
When the _____ ran away, the workmen gave the boy a _____ in its place.
           5.   **6.**
When the _____ broke, a woodcutter gave the boy a _____ in its place.
           7.   **8.**

ROUND-THE-CLOCK ROUND OFF

At the center of each circle, there is a number. Follow each arrow and round the numbers to the nearest hundred, thousand, ten thousand, and hundred thousand.

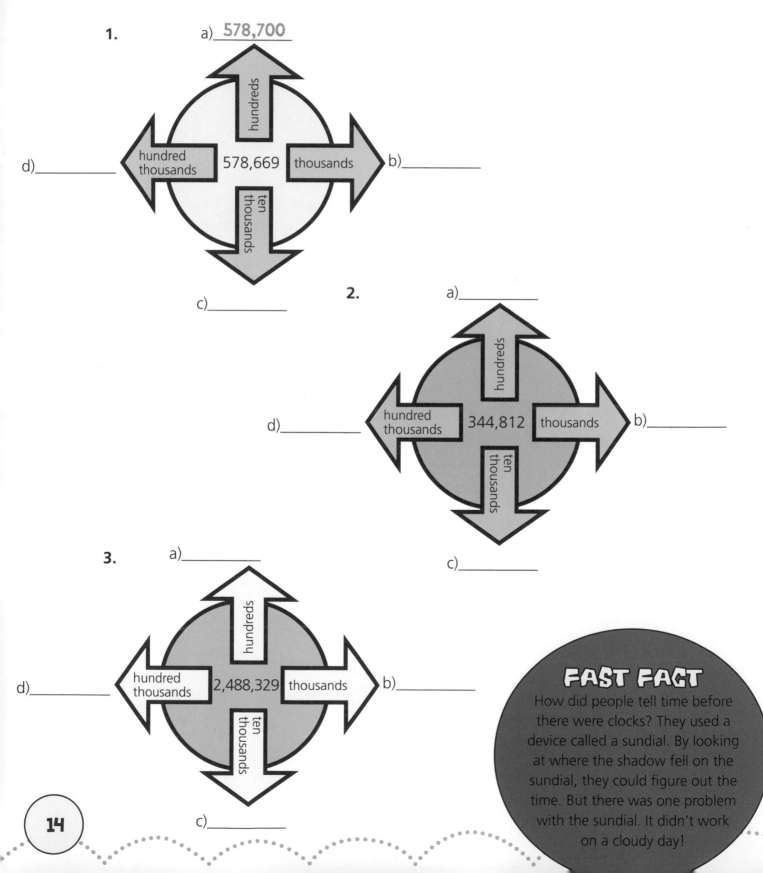

1.

a) 578,700

hundreds

d)_____ hundred thousands | 578,669 | thousands b)_____

ten thousands

c)_____

2.

a)_____

hundreds

d)_____ hundred thousands | 344,812 | thousands b)_____

ten thousands

c)_____

3.

a)_____

hundreds

d)_____ hundred thousands | 2,488,329 | thousands b)_____

ten thousands

c)_____

14

FAST FACT
How did people tell time before there were clocks? They used a device called a sundial. By looking at where the shadow fell on the sundial, they could figure out the time. But there was one problem with the sundial. It didn't work on a cloudy day!

NUTS ABOUT NUMBERS

Write each set of numbers in order from the smallest to the largest.

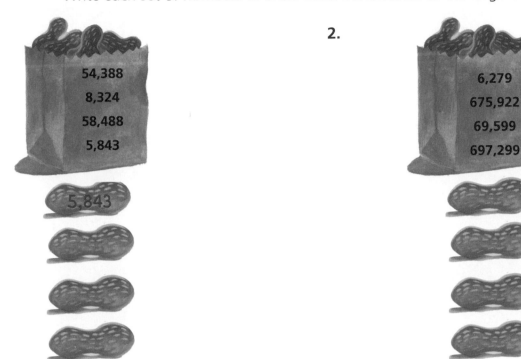

1.

54,388
8,324
58,488
5,843

5,843

2.

6,279
675,922
69,599
697,299

Read each clue and write the numerals in the crossword puzzle.

Across

1. One million, six hundred thousand, four hundred, and fifty

2. Thirty-three thousand, nine hundred, and seventy-two

3. Nine thousand, nine hundred, and sixty-eight

Down

1. Ten thousand, eight hundred, and ninety-nine

4. Three hundred and two thousand, three hundred, and forty-six

5. Four hundred and eighty-nine

6. Seven hundred and eighty-eight

7. One thousand and fifty-two

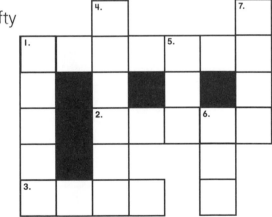

ON YOUR OWN
Find out the year that everyone in your family was born and write it down. Then write each number out in words.

CONSTITUTION CONNECTION

All the words or phrases on the left have to do with the U.S. Constitution. Draw a line to match each one with the correct description on the right.

1. Preamble

2. Articles

3. Amendments

4. Constitutional Convention

5. Articles of Confederation

6. Ratify

7. Separation of Powers

8. Framers

a) The meeting where delegates from all the colonies discussed how the United States should be governed.

b) Changes or additions to the Constitution. The first ten are called the Bill of Rights.

c) To vote on and approve a change to the Constitution.

d) The opening section of the U.S. Constitution. It describes the purpose of the Constitution and the role of the government.

e) There are seven of these in the U.S. Constitution. They explain how the government is structured.

f) The people who wrote and planned the Constitution, like Ben Franklin, James Madison, George Washington, and others.

g) Power is divided up among three branches of government.

h) The United States was governed by this document before the Constitution was written.

FAST FACT

The Constitution was written in secret! The Framers didn't want any outside influences, so they hired armed guards to stand outside the door of their meeting hall.

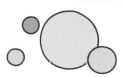

FOREST FIND

Producers are plants that make their own food. **Consumers** can't make their own food, so they eat other plants or animals. **Decomposers** help break down dead plants or animals and return the nutrients to the soil.

Look at the forest scene and find all of the producers, consumers, and decomposers that you can.

Producers

tree

_____

_____

Consumers

_____

_____

_____

Decomposers

_____

_____

_____

ON YOUR OWN

You've got producers, consumers, and decomposers at work right in your own backyard! Take a close look at the plants and animals living in your yard or at a nearby park. Make a list of the producers, consumers, and decomposers you find.

WATER WORDS

Synonyms are words that are alike. **Antonyms** are words that are different. Decide whether the two words inside each lily pad are synonyms or antonyms. List them under the correct column.

Synonyms

_____pond_____,
_____lake_____

_____,
_____

_____,
_____

_____,
_____

Antonyms

_____,
_____

_____,
_____

_____,
_____

_____,
_____

pond, lake

wet, dry

drought, flood

sink, float

drench, soak

deep, shallow

jump, leap

sprinkle, drizzle

Find the synonym for the underlined word in each sentence.

1. We went to the <u>stream</u> to go fishing.
   a) fountain   b) creek   c) underwater

2. I sat on a <u>boulder</u> at the edge of the water.
   a) rock   b) bench   c) chair

3. I waited for a fish to <u>bite</u> on the bait on my fishing pole.
   a) drink   b) nibble   c) dinner

Find the antonym for the underlined word in each sentence.

4. We <u>frequently</u> go to the pool in the summer.
   a) usually   b) seldom   c) always

5. It's <u>rude</u> to splash people when you're swimming.
   a) polite   b) happy   c) careful

6. Everything looks <u>blurry</u> underwater.
   a) foggy   b) rapid   c) clear

ON YOUR OWN
You can make your own fishing pole at home. Have your parents help you find a long pole or stick about 8 feet long. Tie a long piece of string on one end of the pole, and attach a hook on the other end. Now go catch some fish!

18

A SUMMERY SUMMARY

Read about Sarah's summer vacation. Then read the summaries and circle the best one.

Sarah had the best summer vacation ever! She went to Hawaii with her family. Sarah went to the beach every day. She learned how to snorkel and saw lots of pretty fish in all different colors. One day she even saw a sea turtle while she was snorkeling. Sarah's favorite part of the trip happened on the last night. She and her family went to a special dinner and a show called a luau. They watched dancers in hula skirts while they ate dinner. What a treat!

Summary A
Sarah's favorite part of this trip to Hawaii was the luau. The luau included a delicious dinner and a great show. She really liked watching all the hula dancers. What a great way to end this summer vacation!

Summary B
Sarah went to the beach every day when she was in Hawaii. She learned how to snorkel so that she could see all the colorful fish. She even saw a sea turtle one day while she was snorkeling.

Summary C
Sarah went to Hawaii with her family for her summer vacation. She saw colorful fish and a sea turtle while she was snorkeling. Sarah's favorite part of the trip was the luau that she went to on her last night.

On a separate piece of paper write a summary of what you've done so far on your summer vacation. Remember, a summary doesn't include all the details. It just gives the main ideas.

FAST FACT
At a luau there is always a lot of food, like pineapple, rice, roasted pig, and a special pudding called poi. It's no wonder the word *luau* means feast!

PARTY PUNCH

This Party Punch has two recipe cards. Look at the first ingredient. $2\frac{1}{3}$ and $\frac{7}{3}$ are the same, but one is a proper fraction and one is an improper fraction. Convert the fraction for each ingredient to complete the cards.

Proper Punch

$2\frac{1}{3}$ tablespoons strawberry punch powder mix

1. _____ cups sugar

$8\frac{1}{2}$ cups cold water

3. _____ cups orange sherbet

$2\frac{1}{3}$ cups ginger ale

5. _____ cups pineapple juice

$4\frac{3}{4}$ cups orange juice

Improper Punch

$\frac{7}{3}$ tablespoons strawberry punch powder mix

$\frac{5}{4}$ cups sugar

2. _____ cups cold water

$\frac{14}{3}$ cups orange sherbert

4. _____ cups ginger ale

$\frac{19}{4}$ cups pineapple juice

6. _____ cups orange juice

ON YOUR OWN

It's fun to cool off with a frosty glass of punch. Have your parents help you mix together juice, ice cream, and ginger ale to create your own tasty punch!

20

TIC-TAC-TOE

Circle the row where all the fractions and decimals are equal. Don't forget to check the diagonal rows!

1.

.4	$\frac{4}{1}$	$\frac{4}{10}$
.40	$\frac{4}{100}$	.04
$\frac{4}{10}$	.4	$\frac{40}{100}$

(bottom row circled)

2.

.06	$\frac{6}{1}$	$\frac{60}{100}$
$\frac{60}{10}$	6.0	$\frac{6}{10}$
$\frac{6}{100}$	$\frac{6}{10}$	.6

3.

.2	$\frac{1}{2}$	$\frac{2}{10}$
.02	$\frac{2}{100}$	$\frac{20}{1000}$
$\frac{2}{1}$	$\frac{22}{100}$	2.2

4.

.05	$\frac{1}{2}$	5.0
$\frac{5}{10}$	$\frac{5}{100}$	$\frac{20}{1000}$
.5	$\frac{1}{5}$	$\frac{1}{20}$

Write each decimal as a fraction.

5. .3 _____

6. .8 _____

7. .07 _____

Write each fraction as a decimal.

8. $\frac{5}{10}$ _____

9. $\frac{60}{100}$ _____

10. $\frac{4}{100}$ _____

GLOBE TROTTERS

Read the paragraph and label all the parts on the globe.

A globe is a giant sphere, just like the shape of Earth. The **equator** is an imaginary line that goes around the middle of Earth. It divides Earth in half. Think of the equator as a belt that goes around Earth's "waist." Everything above the equator is called the **Northern Hemisphere**. The area below the equator is called the **Southern Hemisphere**.

The **prime meridian** is an imaginary line that divides Earth in half lengthwise, from the **North Pole** to the **South Pole**. Everything to the left of the **prime meridian** is the **Western Hemisphere**. Everything to the right is the **Eastern Hemisphere**.

There are lots of other lines on the globe, too. Lines of **latitude** are horizontal lines that run parallel to the equator. Lines of **longitude** are vertical lines running from north to south. Each line is given a degree. So, if you know the latitude and longitude points, you can find any place on Earth!

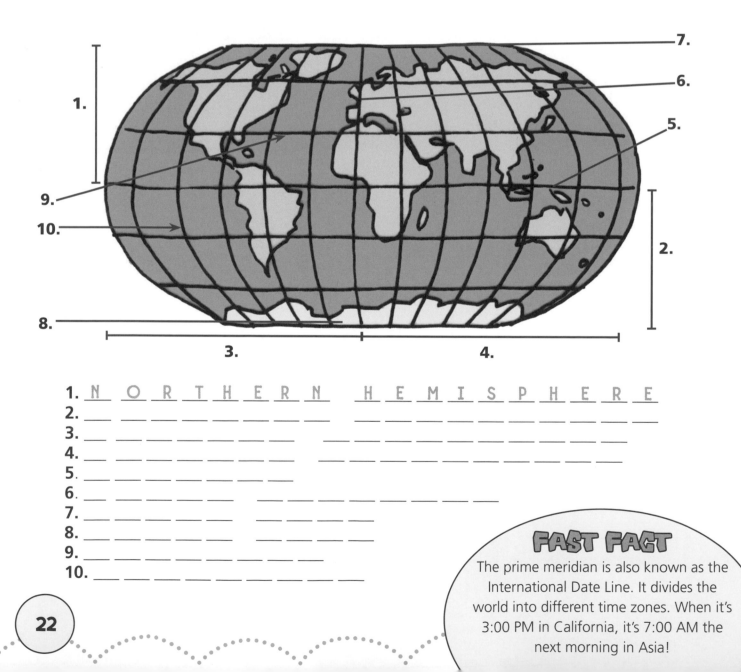

1. <u>N O R T H E R N   H E M I S P H E R E</u>
2. ___ ___ ___ ___ ___ ___ ___   ___ ___ ___ ___ ___ ___ ___ ___
3. ___ ___ ___ ___ ___   ___ ___ ___ ___ ___ ___ ___ ___ ___ ___
4. ___ ___ ___ ___ ___ ___ ___   ___ ___ ___ ___ ___ ___ ___ ___
5. ___ ___ ___ ___ ___ ___ ___
6. ___ ___ ___ ___ ___   ___ ___ ___ ___ ___ ___ ___
7. ___ ___ ___ ___ ___ ___ ___ ___
8. ___ ___ ___ ___ ___   ___ ___ ___ ___
9. ___ ___ ___ ___ ___ ___ ___ ___
10. ___ ___ ___ ___ ___ ___ ___ ___ ___ ___

FAST FACT

The prime meridian is also known as the International Date Line. It divides the world into different time zones. When it's 3:00 PM in California, it's 7:00 AM the next morning in Asia!

NATURE'S NEIGHBORHOOD

An **ecosystem** is a community of living and non-living things and their habitats or environments. Plants, animals, people, air, soil, water, and insects are all part of an ecosystem. Plants and animals are dependent on each other for survival, so everything in an ecosystem is dependant on something else within the ecosystem.

Study this picture of an ecosystem. Then answer the questions below.

ON YOUR OWN
Study the ecosystem that exists in your own backyard or at a nearby park. Make a list of all the plants and animals and show how they're dependent on one another!

Make a list of some of the animals in this ecosystem and their habitats.

Animal	Habitat
earthworm	mud
_____	_____
_____	_____
_____	_____

Complete the sentences to show how everything in an ecosystem is dependent on something else within the ecosystem.

A ___duck___ depends on ___plants___ for ___food___ .
A _____ depends on _____ for _____ .
A _____ needs _____ to _____ .
A _____ needs _____ to _____ .
A _____ uses a _____ for _____ .

DIGGING UP ROOTS

Write each word from the garden under its root, below. Then use a dictionary to find one more word that has each root. Write a definition for each word.

1. port (carry)

transport : to carry from one place to another

_____ : _____

_____ : _____

2. aud (hear)

_____ : _____

_____ : _____

_____ : _____

3. auto (self)

_____ : _____

_____ : _____

_____ : _____

4. graph / gram (to write)

_____ : _____

_____ : _____

_____ : _____

ON YOUR OWN

Dictionary entries include notes about the word root at the end of the definition. Look up some of your favorite words and find out what their roots are!

BITE INTO THAT

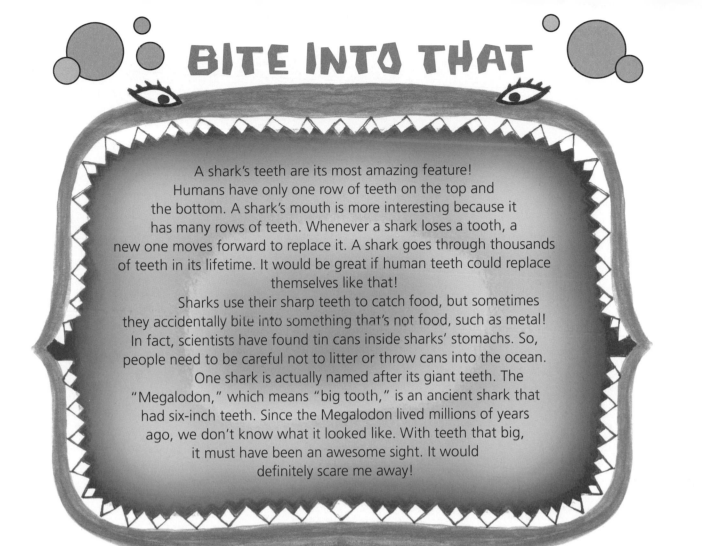

A shark's teeth are its most amazing feature! Humans have only one row of teeth on the top and the bottom. A shark's mouth is more interesting because it has many rows of teeth. Whenever a shark loses a tooth, a new one moves forward to replace it. A shark goes through thousands of teeth in its lifetime. It would be great if human teeth could replace themselves like that!

Sharks use their sharp teeth to catch food, but sometimes they accidentally bite into something that's not food, such as metal! In fact, scientists have found tin cans inside sharks' stomachs. So, people need to be careful not to litter or throw cans into the ocean. One shark is actually named after its giant teeth. The "Megalodon," which means "big tooth," is an ancient shark that had six-inch teeth. Since the Megalodon lived millions of years ago, we don't know what it looked like. With teeth that big, it must have been an awesome sight. It would definitely scare me away!

Read through the paragraph and find sentences that give **facts** and sentences that express the author's **opinions**. Write the sentences below.

Facts

_____

_____

_____

Opinions

_____

_____

_____

_____

FAST FACT

Shark teeth also give us information about the past! Old shark teeth sink to the ocean floor, and the sand preserves them for millions of years. Scientists can study these old teeth and learn about ancient sharks.

Which sentence best describes the author's attitude?
a) Sharks are so dumb that they eat tin cans by accident!
b) Shark teeth are interesting and tell us a lot about these great animals.
c) Humans would be better off if they had teeth as sharp as sharks.

MULTIPLICATION MARATHON

Multiply to solve each problem. See how fast you can finish all the problems!

1. 452
  x 5
  2260

2. 235
  x 6

3. 338
  x 4

4. 12
  x 12

5. 58
  x 13

6. 45
  x 22

7. 231
  x 14

8. 664
  x 11

9. 173
  x 25

10. 525
  x 10

11. 226
  x 34

12. 709
  x 82

FAST FACT
How long is a real marathon? The official distance of a marathon course is 26.2 miles!

DIVISION DAYS

Solve each division problem and find the answer at the bottom. Some of the answers have remainders. Write the letter on the line and you'll solve the riddle!

S	L	E	Z	W	A	O
4)168	7)321	5)982	2)308	9)376	8)387	6)480
N	**I**	**D**	**T**	**S**	**A**	**A**
4)185	7)406	2)522	3)752	8)168	4)565	5)75

Why was the calendar so confused?

It ____ ____ ____   ____ ____ ____ ____   ____ ____   ____
   41 R7   15   42   45 R6   80   21   250 R2   58   46 R1   141 R1

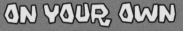

____ ____ ____ ____.
261 48 R3 154 196 R2

ON YOUR OWN
Keep track of all your summer activities on a calendar. Each day, write down where you went and what you did. At the end of the summer, you'll be amazed at all the things you did!

POSTCARD FROM THE PAST

Think about the history of the state where you live. Choose a specific time in the past and imagine what it was like to live during that time. Write a postcard to someone describing what life is like in your state. You can use an encyclopedia or another reference book for help.

Use these questions to help you think about the history of your state.

Who lived in your state before Columbus arrived?

Why did people begin moving to your state, and how did they get there?

How did your state gain statehood?

Were there any wars or conflicts that took place in your state?

What kinds of jobs did people have?

Where did most people live?

What are some special features in your state?

FAST FACT

Do you know what a state historian is? This is a special person in each state whose job it is to write down the history of the state. He or she keeps track of important historical events, documents, places, and people in your state!

ROCKY RIDDLES

Read each riddle and find the answer in the box. Write the answer to the riddle on the line.

calcite	metamorphic	feldspar
igneous	sedimentary	quartz

1.

I am a mineral with six-sided crystals.
I am so hard, I can scratch steel.
I am used in jewelry and glass.

quartz

2.

I am so soft, I can be scratched with
a penny. I am white, yellow, or sometimes
transparent. I am used in toothpaste,
chewing gum, glue, and soap.

_____

3.

I am the most common of all minerals.
I have flat sides. I come in many colors,
like pink, white, and green.

_____

4.

I come from volcanoes!
When lava cools, it hardens into rock.
That's how I'm made.

_____

5.

I have many layers called strata.
Each layer is made from tiny rocks
that formed together.
That's how I'm made.

_____

6.

I am a rock that has undergone a change.
Heat and pressure turn me into something
new. That's how I'm made.

_____

ON YOUR OWN

Collect rocks from your own
backyard and neighborhood.
Classify all the rocks you find and
sort them into groups!

THE SUMMER OF CLUBS

Read the story. Then answer the questions.

Scott and Steve played together every summer. Then one summer, Steve's cousin Henry came to visit. Scott was worried that Steve would spend all of his time with Henry, so Scott came up with a plan to keep Steve to himself.

Scott decided to start the Tree House Club. He knew that Henry was afraid of heights, so he planned to have the club meet in a tree house. Scott asked Steve to join the club.

"That sounds great," said Steve. "But my cousin Henry won't be able to climb into the tree house. Can he still be in the club?"

"Sorry," Scott said, "but those are the club rules. If he doesn't want to go in the tree house, then he can't be in the club. Besides, you don't have to do everything with Henry."

Steve agreed to join the club. He had a lot of fun playing with Scott in the tree house, but Henry felt left out. Steve started to feel guilty about leaving his cousin all alone.

Steve came up with a plan, too. He and Henry started the Island Club. They planned to swim across the lake and have meetings on an island. They asked Scott to join.

"But I don't know how to swim," Scott said. "Can I still be in the club?"

"Sorry, but no," said Steve. "Those are the club rules."

Steve and Henry had a lot of fun swimming to the island. Scott looked on sadly. Now he understood what it was like to be left out.

"I have an idea," he told Steve and Henry. "Let's start a new club together. We'll call it the Fun Club! The only rule is that we all have fun together and don't leave anybody out."

Steve and Henry agreed. In fact, they found that they could have even more fun with three people!

Write some words that describe each character.

Scott	Steve	Henry
_____	_____	_____
_____	_____	_____
_____	_____	_____

FAST FACT

In some parts of the world, people actually live in tree houses. Sometimes swamplands are too wet to support a house. Or, if there is dry ground, a house can get washed away with seasonal floods. So people build their homes up high in the treetops!

Refer to the story on page 30 to fill in the information.

The Tree House Club

1. Club Members: _____

2. Who started this club and why?
   _____ started the club because _____
   _____.

3. Club Rule: _____
   What happened because of the rule?
   _____
   _____

The Island Club

4. Club Members: _____

5. Who started this club and why?
   _____ started the club because _____
   _____.

6. Club Rule: _____
   What happened because of the rule?
   _____
   _____

The Fun Club

7. Club Members: _____

8. Who started this club and why?
   _____ started the club because _____
   _____.

9. Club Rule: _____
   What happened because of the rule?
   _____
   _____

10. Circle all of the misspelled words below.

| finally | quartor | again | becaus | diffrent |
| favrite | untill | realy | upstairs | every |

LAURA'S LUNCH

Plug each set of numbers into the equation. If the number pair makes a true equation, color the box. If not, leave the box blank. Try all the number pairs to figure out which meal Laura had for lunch!

$$3 + a = b$$

a = 4 b = 7 3 + 4 = 7	a = 3 b = 6	a = 3 b = 9	a = 5 b = 15
a = 2 b = 6	a = 12 b = 15	a = 10 b = 13	a = 11 b = 15
a = 2 b = 1	a = 8 b = 12	a = 6 b = 9	a = 1 b = 4

$$10 - a = b$$

$$a + 7 = b$$

1. If a = 5, b = __5__
2. If a = 9, b = ____
3. If b = 4, a = ____
4. If b = 7, a = ____

5. If a = 3, b = ____
6. If a = 7, b = ____
7. If b = 9, a = ____
8. If b = 20, a = ____

FOLLOW THE SIGNS

Solve each equation. Remember to do the problem inside the parentheses first.

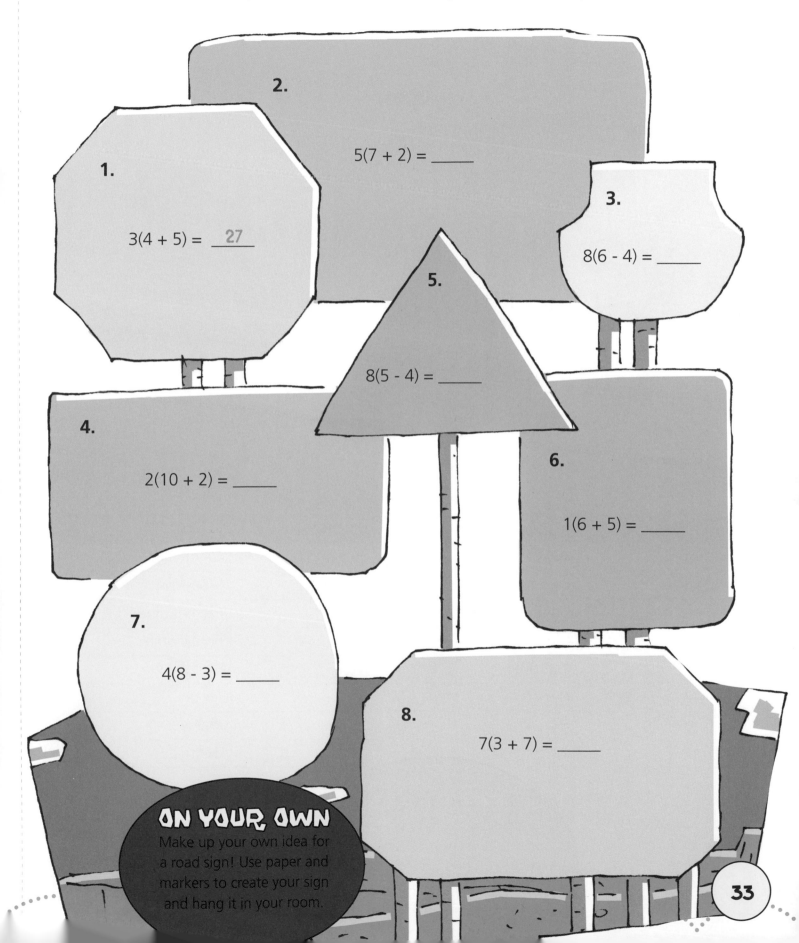

1. $3(4 + 5) =$ ___27___

2. $5(7 + 2) =$ _____

3. $8(6 - 4) =$ _____

4. $2(10 + 2) =$ _____

5. $8(5 - 4) =$ _____

6. $1(6 + 5) =$ _____

7. $4(8 - 3) =$ _____

8. $7(3 + 7) =$ _____

ON YOUR OWN

Make up your own idea for a road sign! Use paper and markers to create your sign and hang it in your room.

TIME OUT

The United States is divided into four time zones. Each time zone is one hour apart. When it's 1:00 in Pacific time, it's 2:00 Mountain time, 3:00 Central time, and 4:00 Eastern time. Look at the map, then fill in the chart.

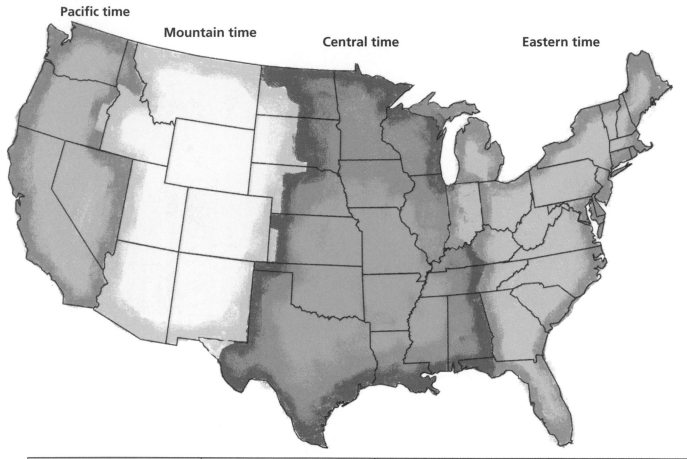

	When it's	In	Then it's	In
1.	11:00 AM	Pacific time	1:00 PM	Central time
2.	5:00 PM	Eastern time		Mountain time
3.	8:00 AM	Central time		Eastern time
4.	Noon	Mountain time		Pacific time
5.	3:00 PM	California		Florida
6.	8:00 AM	New York		Texas
7.	10:00 PM	Nevada		Maine
8.	Midnight	Illinois		Georgia

FAST FACT

The United States isn't the only place that has different time zones. In fact, the entire globe is divided into time zones. There are 24 time zones, and each zone is one hour apart.

IT'S SHOCKING!

Read about the difference between static electricity and current electricity. Then find examples of each type of electricity in the picture and list them below.

Static Electricity

A buildup of electrons
Stays in one place and jumps to an object
Does not need a circuit
Examples: Lightning; when you drag your feet across carpet and touch something

Current Electricity

Steady flow of electrons
Needs a conductor (like a wire)
Needs a circuit
Examples: Batteries; outlet plugs

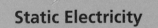

Static Electricity

_____
_____
_____

Current Electricity

_____
_____
_____

ON YOUR OWN

Look around your house and make a list of all the things you use that need electricity. Then imagine what life would be like with no electricity! Write a story about a day without any electrical appliances.

WORDS ON WHEELS

Add a prefix and a suffix to complete each word.

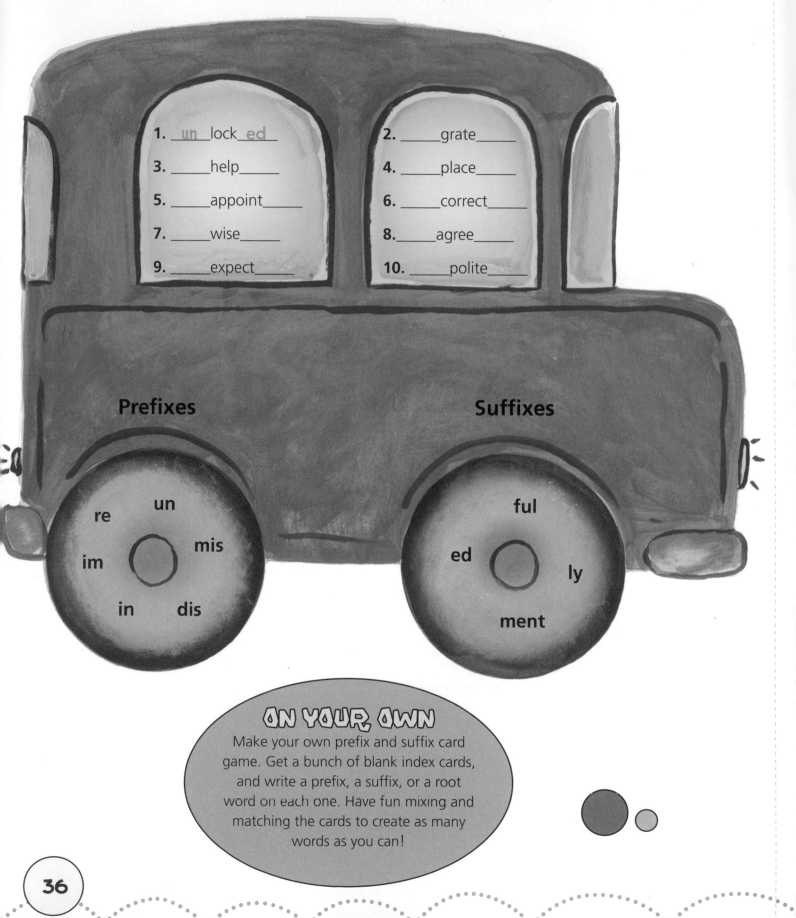

1. __un__ lock __ed__
2. _____ grate _____
3. _____ help _____
4. _____ place _____
5. _____ appoint _____
6. _____ correct _____
7. _____ wise _____
8. _____ agree _____
9. _____ expect _____
10. _____ polite _____

Prefixes

re   un   mis   im   in   dis

Suffixes

ful   ed   ly   ment

ON YOUR OWN
Make your own prefix and suffix card game. Get a bunch of blank index cards, and write a prefix, a suffix, or a root word on each one. Have fun mixing and matching the cards to create as many words as you can!

AMAZING AMERICAN WOMEN

Abigail Adams

Abigail Adams was an important leader in America's fight for independence. Abigail wanted America to break away from England and become its own country. Her husband, John Adams, was often away helping with the American Revolution. Abigail raised the children and ran the farm by herself. She wrote many letters to her husband, sharing her opinions about independence. She also felt strongly about improving the treatment of women during this time. When John was helping to write the nation's new constitution, Abigail wrote to him to remind him about the importance of women's rights. Abigail and John both enjoyed reading and writing about politics. John was the vice president to George Washington and then was elected as the second president of the United States. Abigail was a partner to and a supporter of her husband.

Mercy Otis Warren

Mercy Otis Warren helped support the Revolutionary War through her writing. Mercy believed strongly that America should gain independence from England. She became a patriot writer, and she wrote plays, poems, articles, and books that supported independence. Mercy also felt passionately about women's rights. She thought it was wrong that women were not seen as equal to men during this time. Mercy married James Warren, and together they enjoyed reading, writing, and discussing politics. James was elected to the Massachusetts House of Representatives during the Revolution. Mercy supported her husband and continued to write about independence.

FAST FACT
Abigail Adams and Mercy Otis Warren were actually friends and often wrote letters to each other.

Compare and contrast these two women by filling in the diagram. In the middle of the diagram, write some things that Abigail Adams and Mercy Otis Warren have in common. In the other parts, write about things that are unique to each woman.

Abigail Adams   **Mercy Otis Warren**

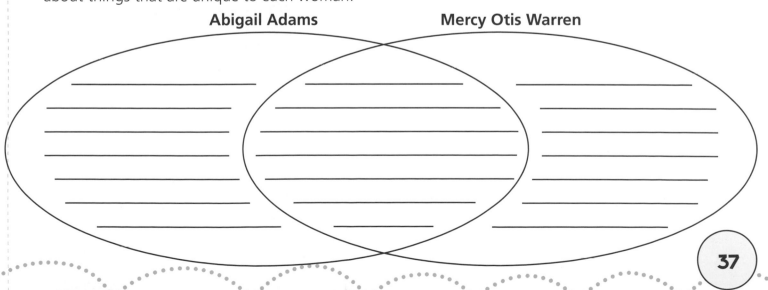

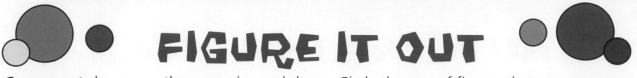

FIGURE IT OUT

Congruent shapes are the same size and shape. Circle the sets of figures that are congruent.

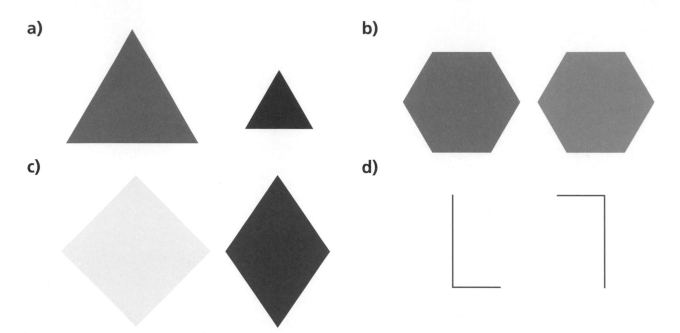

a)

b)

c)

d)

Symmetry means that a shape is made of two sides that are exactly the same. Circle the figures that are symmetrical.

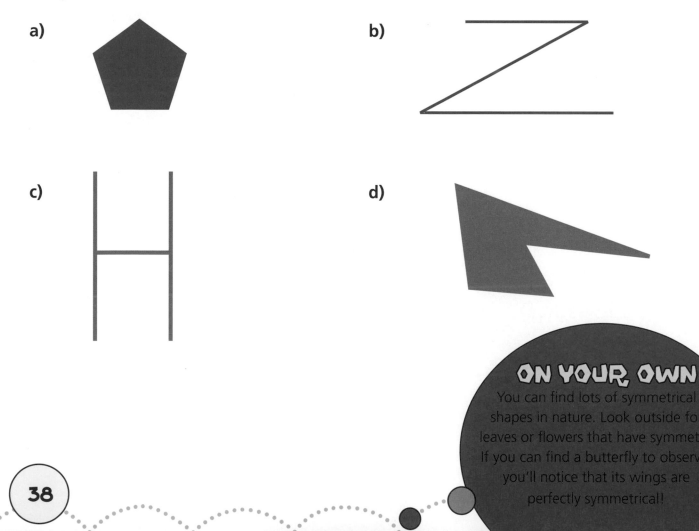

a)

b)

c)

d)

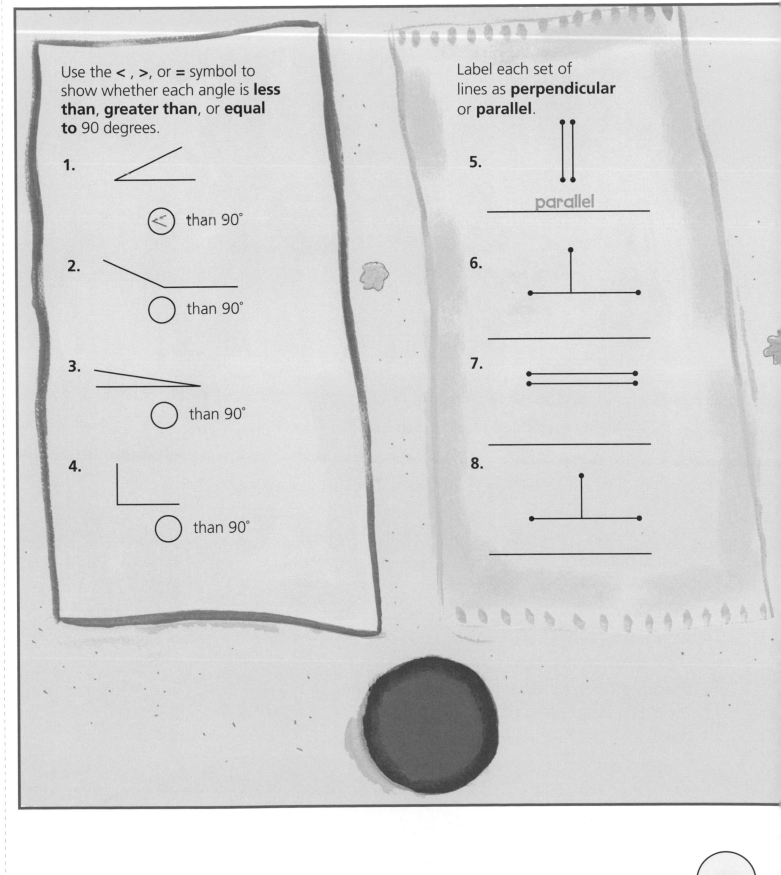

Use the **<** , **>**, or **=** symbol to show whether each angle is **less than**, **greater than**, or **equal to** 90 degrees.

1. $<$ than 90°

2. ◯ than 90°

3. ◯ than 90°

4. ◯ than 90°

Label each set of lines as **perpendicular** or **parallel**.

5. parallel

6. _____

7. _____

8. _____

BRANCHING OUT

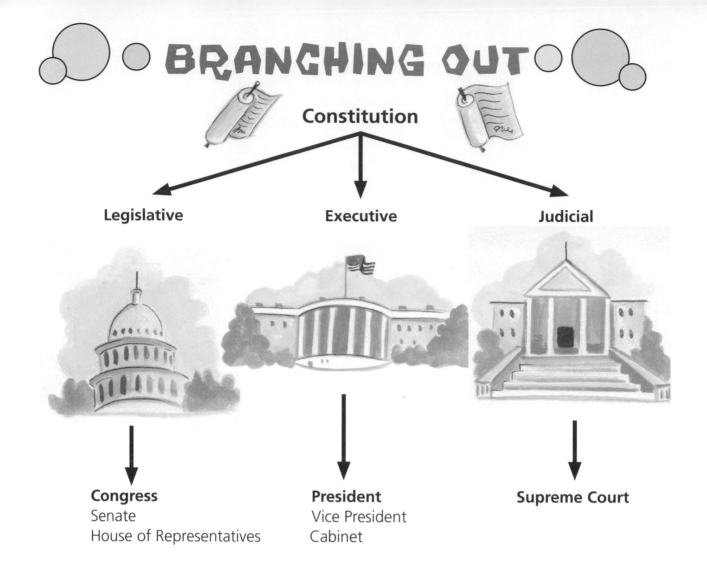

Constitution

Legislative | Executive | Judicial

Congress
Senate
House of Representatives

President
Vice President
Cabinet

Supreme Court

Connect each definition with the correct word. Use the diagram above for help.

1. A group of people who advise and help the president.
2. A body of lawmakers made up of the Senate and the House of Representatives together.
3. The branch of government that makes up the court system.
4. The head of the executive branch.
5. The document that explains how the government is structured.
6. The branch of government that makes laws through congress.
7. The president is the head of this branch.
8. The highest court in the nation.

a) Constitution
b) Legislative
c) Executive
d) Judicial
e) Supreme Court
f) President
g) Congress
h) Cabinet

FAST FACT
After being ruled by England for so long, the Founding Fathers didn't want any one person to have too much power. They created the three separate government branches to spread the power around. This is called separation of powers.

VOLCANO VOCABULARY

Find the word that completes each sentence.

magma

lava

crust

dormant

active

mantle

erupt

pressure

What makes a volcano 1) ___erupt___? It all starts deep within the Earth. The top layer of Earth is called the 2) _____. Below the crust is a layer of hot rock called the 3) _____. The heat and 4) _____in the mantle cause the rock to melt into a liquid. This hot melted rock, called 5) _____, bursts through a crack in the Earth's crust. When the magma flows down the side of the volcano, we call it 6) _____. A volcano that has erupted before or that continues to erupt is called an 7) _____ volcano. Sometimes, when lava cools and hardens, it plugs up the volcano and it stops erupting. When this happens, the volcano is called a sleeping, or 8) _____, volcano.

ON YOUR OWN

You can make your own erupting volcano. Form a hollow mountain shape out of clay, making sure to leave the top open. Place a few tablespoons of baking soda inside the volcano. Then pour some vinegar inside, and watch your volcano erupt!

GREETING CARD GUESS

A **simile** is a comparison using the words *like* or *as*.
A **metaphor** is a comparison that does not use *like* or *as*.
The **personification** of a word means giving it human qualities.

Look at each card. Decide if the card's message is an example of simile, metaphor, or personification.
Then create your own greeting card and use **figurative language** to write a message!

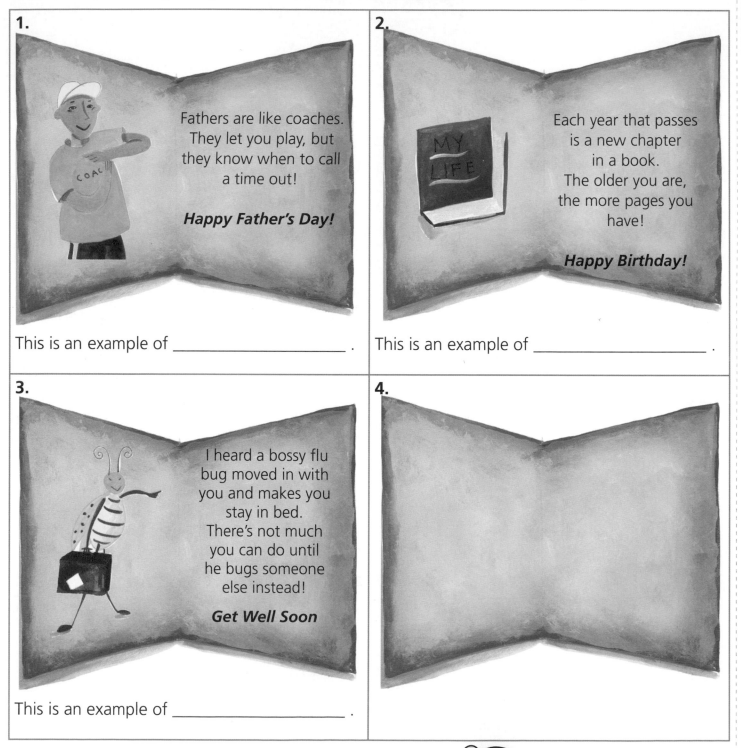

1.

Fathers are like coaches.
They let you play, but
they know when to call
a time out!

Happy Father's Day!

This is an example of _____ .

2.

Each year that passes
is a new chapter
in a book.
The older you are,
the more pages you
have!

Happy Birthday!

This is an example of _____ .

3.

I heard a bossy flu
bug moved in with
you and makes you
stay in bed.
There's not much
you can do until
he bugs someone
else instead!

Get Well Soon

This is an example of _____ .

4.

ELEVATOR OUT OF ORDER

This story is out of order. Number each group of sentences to show the correct story sequence.

a) _____ By the time she got to the top, she was exhausted. She found her father's office and walked inside. He was so excited to see her.

b) _____ Just as she had finished preparing the dinner, her dad called. He had to work late at his office and he couldn't get home in time for his birthday dinner.

c) _____ "I've come to bring you your birthday dinner," Amy told her dad. "How wonderful," her dad said. "What did you bring?"

d) _____ Amy always did something special for her dad on his birthday. One year, she decided to make her dad a special birthday dinner.

e) _____ When they got to the office building, Amy ran inside with the food packages. She stopped when she saw a big sign on the elevator door. It said, "Elevator Out of Order."

f) _____ Amy and her dad walked down the fourteen flights of stairs. They found the packages of food by the broken elevator.

g) _____ Then Amy had an idea for a birthday surprise. "If Dad can't come to his birthday dinner, then his birthday dinner will go to him!" she told her mom. Amy's mom drove her to his office so that they could drop off the dinner.

h) _____ Amy's father's office was on the fourteenth floor! That's a lot of stairs, but Amy was determined. She started the long trek up the stairs.

i) _____ Just then, her dad's boss approached the elevator. "It looks like the elevator is broken," he said. "You can't walk up fourteen flights of stairs. I guess you can go home for the night!" So Amy, her dad, and the special birthday dinner all went home together.

j) _____ "Oh no!" Amy looked around and couldn't find the packages of food. She realized that she must have left them down by the elevator.

ON YOUR OWN
Write your own story on a large piece of paper, then cut up the paper into several pieces. Have a friend read your story and put the story pieces back in the correct order.

At the family reunion, 20 people in the family voted on what activities to do. Fill in the blanks to show the percentage of people that voted for each activity.

1. 10 people wanted to go swimming. $\frac{10}{20} = \frac{50}{100} = \underline{50}$ %

2. 6 people wanted to go horseback riding. $\frac{6}{20} = \frac{30}{100} = \underline{}$%

3. 4 people wanted to go hiking. $\frac{4}{20} = \frac{20}{100} = \underline{}$%

4. 2 people wanted to go fishing. $\frac{2}{20} = \frac{10}{100} = \underline{}$%

The family reunion lasted for five days, but not everyone could be there every day. This chart shows how many people were there each day.

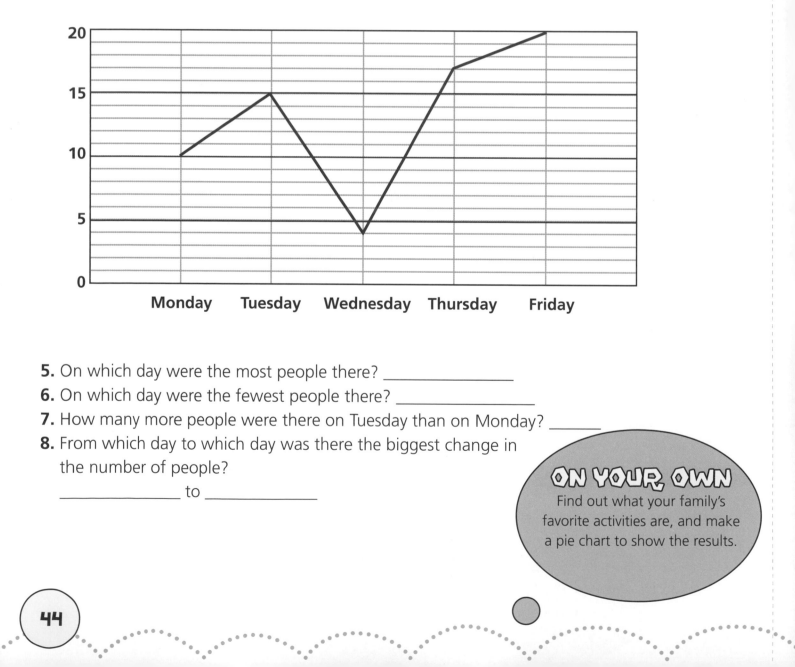

5. On which day were the most people there? _____

6. On which day were the fewest people there? _____

7. How many more people were there on Tuesday than on Monday? _____

8. From which day to which day was there the biggest change in the number of people?

_____ to _____

ON YOUR OWN
Find out what your family's favorite activities are, and make a pie chart to show the results.

IT TAKES COORDINATION

Graph the ordered pairs in the box on the grid. Connect the points as you go.

| 1,5 | 4,6 | 5,10 | 6,6 | 10,5 | 7,4 | 9,1 | 5,3 | 1,1 | 3,4 |

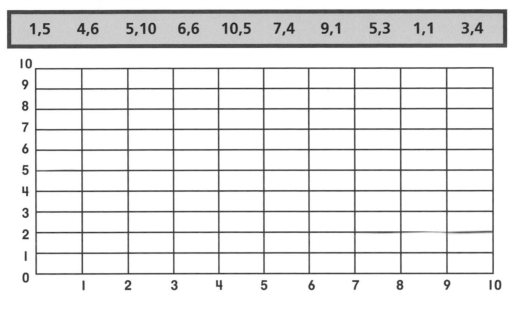

The ordered pairs on the grid below show the positions of players on a baseball field. Write the coordinates for each position in the chart.

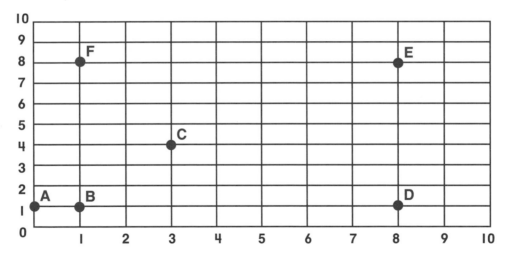

Player	Label	Ordered Pair
Catcher	A	0,1
Batter	B	___
Pitcher	C	___
1st Base	D	___
2nd Base	E	___
3rd Base	F	___

THOMAS JEFFERSON

Read the story. Then fill in the dates and missing information in the timeline.

Thomas Jefferson, the third president of the United States, was a politician, patriot, writer, inventor, and builder. As a young boy growing up in Virginia, Thomas had many interests. In 1768, at the young age of 26, he started building a plantation called Monticello. He enjoyed filling his home with his own inventions.

Throughout his life, Thomas Jefferson always fought to protect America's freedom. He was at the second Continental Congress in 1776, where he was asked to write the Declaration of Independence. This important document was the beginning of the Revolutionary War.

Jefferson went on to serve the country in many ways. As a member of Congress in 1783, he helped create the American money system. Then, from 1796 to 1801, he was vice president to John Adams. In 1801, Thomas Jefferson was elected president. In 1803, he bought an important piece of land from France. This is known as the Louisiana Purchase.

In 1809, Jefferson retired and returned to Monticello, but even after retiring, he continued to help his country. In 1819, he founded and built the University of Virginia. By the end of his life, Jefferson had spent more than fifty years serving his country!

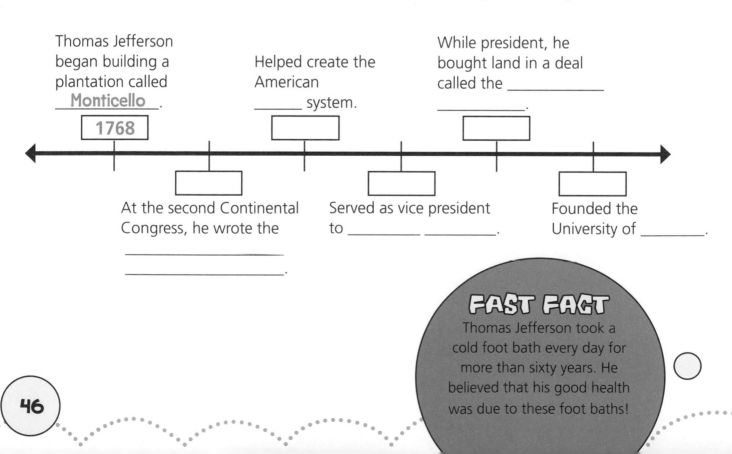

Thomas Jefferson began building a plantation called ___Monticello___.

1768

Helped create the American _____ system.

While president, he bought land in a deal called the _____ _____.

At the second Continental Congress, he wrote the _____ _____.

Served as vice president to _____ _____.

Founded the University of _____.

FAST FACT

Thomas Jefferson took a cold foot bath every day for more than sixty years. He believed that his good health was due to these foot baths!

CROSSWORD PUZZLE

Erosion is the process by which material is worn away. Each word in the puzzle is related to erosion. Use the clues to complete the puzzle.

Across
1. A landslide of snow moving quickly down a mountain side
2. A large body of ice that slowly moves, taking pieces of land along with it
3. The force that pulls everything downward, causing rain and soil to run down a slope

Down
1. Polluted rainwater that can burn plants and corrode rocks
4. A sudden rush of mud and debris falling down a slope
5. The wearing down of rocks, soil, or land by nature's forces
6. Small particles, like dirt, that can be scattered by wind and water
7. Hard, solid masses that can be worn down by wind and water

A V A L A N C H E

ON YOUR OWN
Do a simple experiment to see how acid rain erodes rocks. Fill a cup with lemon juice or vinegar, and drop a piece of chalk inside. Watch what happens to the chalk over the next few days as the acid erodes it.

SALLY'S SCENES

Setting is the time and place in which something happens. **Mood** is the feeling or emotion in a story. Read each scene and write a word to describe the setting. Then choose the word that best describes the mood.

> **Mood Words**
>
> happy   serious
>
> frightening   hopeful

1. Sally had lost control of her bike! She gripped the handlebars tightly as the bike sped downhill toward Mrs. Grady's house. Sally screamed and shut her eyes as her bike crashed into Mrs. Grady's fence. She flew off her bike and landed by the flower pots. One of the pots broke into pieces and the plants were crushed.

      Setting: _Mrs. Grady's house_____
      Mood: _frightening_____

2. The hospital room was cold and gray. Sally lay on the stiff exam table while the doctor bandaged her aching foot. Sally's mom sat next to her, looking worried.

  "One of Mrs. Grady's flower pots was destroyed," her mom said. "We'll need to replace it for her."

      Setting: _____
      Mood: _____

3. When Sally woke up the next morning, her foot was feeling a little better. Mrs. Grady's flower pot was in her bedroom, and the pieces had been glued back together. The plant was still damaged, but the leaves were perking back up.

  "Mrs. Grady and I repaired the pot," Sally's mom said. "It's almost as good as new!"

      Setting: _____
      Mood: _____

4. Sally still couldn't walk, but she could sit in the sunshine and help Mrs. Grady with her blooming garden. The pot was back in one piece, and the plant was strong and healthy again. Sally had a healthy glow on her face, too.

  "All it takes is a little care and some sunshine to make something as good as new," Mrs. Grady said with a smile.

      Setting: _____
      Mood: _____

MR. FIX IT

There is one mistake in each sentence. Find the mistakes and rewrite the correct paragraph on a separate sheet of paper.

Look for sentences
that need commas or
punctuation at the end of the sentence.
Check to make sure words are capitalized.
Find words that need apostrophes. Check
verbs for the correct tense and subject/verb agreement.

1) this summer, my dad wanted to fix up our house. **2)** He read an article in "home improvement" magazine about how to do repairs. **3)** We didnt have many tools at our house. **4)** My dad had a saw a hammer and some nails. **5)** We tried to do the repairs, but my dads tools were too old. **6)** We werent able to fix anything correctly. **7)** So I decided it were time to ask for some help. **8)** I looked through the chicago gazette for an advertisement. **9)** I saw an ad for a man named Mr. Fix It, so I writed him a letter. **10)** I told him to come to 355 mulberry street and help us with our repairs. **11)** A few days later mr. Fix It showed up at our house. **12)** He new how to do just about everything. **13)** He have all kinds of great tools, so the job was fast and easy. **14)** What would we have done without Mr. Fix It **15)** Within a few day's, everything was fixed. **16)** The only problem was that my dad's old tools was all broken!

SNACK SHACK

Add, subtract, multiply, or divide to solve the problems.

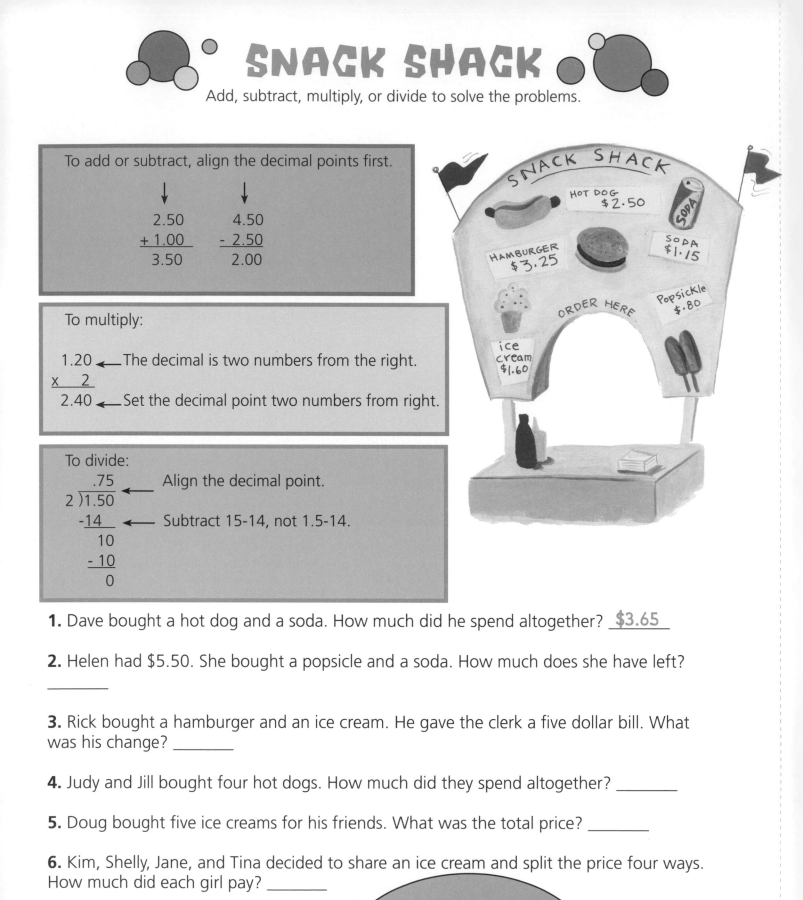

To add or subtract, align the decimal points first.

$$2.50$$
$$+ 1.00$$
$$3.50$$

$$4.50$$
$$- 2.50$$
$$2.00$$

To multiply:

1.20 ← The decimal is two numbers from the right.
x   2
2.40 ← Set the decimal point two numbers from right.

To divide:

```
    .75      Align the decimal point.
2 )1.50
  -14        Subtract 15-14, not 1.5-14.
   10
  - 10
    0
```

1. Dave bought a hot dog and a soda. How much did he spend altogether? _$3.65_

2. Helen had $5.50. She bought a popsicle and a soda. How much does she have left? _____

3. Rick bought a hamburger and an ice cream. He gave the clerk a five dollar bill. What was his change? _____

4. Judy and Jill bought four hot dogs. How much did they spend altogether? _____

5. Doug bought five ice creams for his friends. What was the total price? _____

6. Kim, Shelly, Jane, and Tina decided to share an ice cream and split the price four ways. How much did each girl pay? _____

ON YOUR OWN

Pretend that you have $5.00 to spend at your favorite candy store. Figure out how many different things you can buy without going over $5.00.

FAVORITE FOODS

This pie chart shows kids' favorite snacks at the Snack Shack.

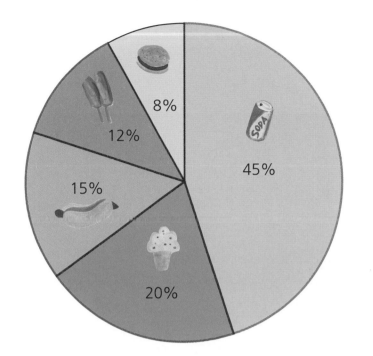

8%

12%

15%

45%

20%

To change a percentage to a decimal, set the decimal point two numbers from the right.

55% = .55. = .55

Change each percentage to a decimal.

1. 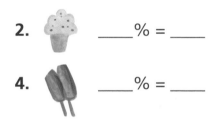 __45__ % = _.45_

2. __ % = __

3. __ % = __

4. __ % = __

5. __ % = __

20 kids were asked about their favorite snack. 45% said it was soda. How many kids is 45% of 20?
45% = .45
```
    20
x  .45
   100
   800
  9.00  →  remember to set the decimal point
```
9 kids said soda was their favorite snack.

6. 20% of the 20 kids said ice cream was their favorite snack.
How many kids is that? _____ kids
```
    20
x  .20
```

ON YOUR OWN
Take your own poll of the kids in your neighborhood and find out what their favorite snacks are. Figure out the percentages for each snack, and make a pie chart to show the results!

A COUNTRY OF MANY NATIONS

This map shows where some Native American tribes were originally settled. The number shows the current population of that tribe.

Crow 9,117

Paiute 9,705

Shoshone 12,026

Ute 10,385   Sioux 153,360

Iriquois 80,822

Navajo 298,197   Cherokee 729,533

Apache 57,060

Creek 40,223

Comanche 19,376

Write the names of the tribes in alphabetical order.

1. _____Apache_____
2. _____
3. _____
4. _____
5. _____
6. _____
7. _____
8. _____
9. _____
10. _____
11. _____

Write the tribes in order from greatest to smallest population.

12. _____
13. _____
14. _____
15. _____
16. _____
17. _____
18. _____
19. _____
20. _____
21. _____
22. _____

ON YOUR OWN

Find out where your parents and grandparents grew up and where all your relatives live now. Find a map you can write on and label it with the names of your relatives.

AMAZING ATOMS

All matter is made up of **atoms**. Each atom has a center, called a **nucleus**. There are tiny particles called **protons** and **neutrons** in the nucleus. Surrounding the nucleus are other particles called **electrons**.

Atoms can't be seen without a microscope, but scientists have been able to discover many different types of atoms, or elements. Each element has a different number of protons, neutrons, and electrons. All of the different atoms, or elements, are on a chart called the Periodic Table.

The Periodic Table shows the number of electrons in each element.

This model of carbon shows the 6 electrons.

Count the number of electrons on each atom model. Connect it with the correct element.

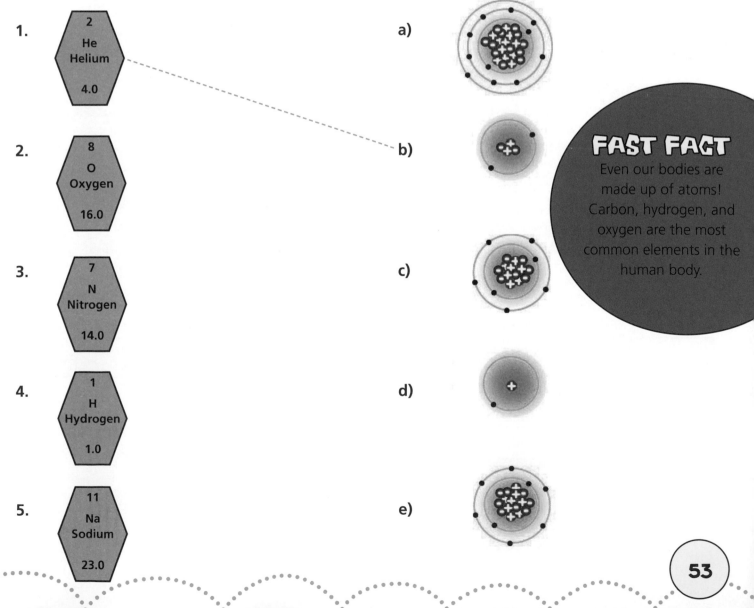

1. 2 He Helium 4.0

2. 8 O Oxygen 16.0

3. 7 N Nitrogen 14.0

4. 1 H Hydrogen 1.0

5. 11 Na Sodium 23.0

a)

b)

c)

d)

e)

FAST FACT
Even our bodies are made up of atoms! Carbon, hydrogen, and oxygen are the most common elements in the human body.

FUN IN THE SUN

Passage A	Passage B
Don't get burned! A sunburn can make you miss out on summer fun. That's why you need Super Summer Sunscreen. It lasts for a really long time and it doesn't wash off in the water. So you can spend all day splashing around with your friends and never get burned. If you want to have a super summer, tell your parents to buy Super Summer Sunscreen for you!	It's important to keep your kids safe from the Sun during the summer. The Sun's rays can cause damage to the skin and leave a painful sunburn. Here are some tips to prevent your kids from getting burned this summer. • Make sure they put on sunscreen every day. • Have them wear a hat or visor and sunglasses. • The Sun's rays are most damaging between 10:00 AM and 2:00 PM, so be extra careful during this time.

Read each phrase and decide if it describes passage A or B. Put a check in the correct column.

	A	B
1. An advertisement	✓	
2. An informative paragraph with tips		
3. Wants to inform the reader about preventing sunburn		
4. Wants the reader to buy a certain sunscreen		
5. Aimed at kids		
6. Aimed at parents		

THE QUOTE BOAT

Read the passage below and add quotation marks to the sentences that need them.

Put quotation marks around:

A speaker's words:
"Let's go sailing," Sam said.
Titles of magazines, songs, and poems:
Pam reads "Sail Away" magazine.

Pam and Sam liked to go sailing. One day they took their sailboat out on the water, but there was no wind to push the sail.

Oh no! said Pam. We'll never be able to sail without some wind.

We just need to be patient and wait for the wind, Sam said.

So Pam and Sam waited and waited. When there was still no wind, Pam said, We can't wait around all day. We need to do something.

What can we do? Sam asked. We can't control the wind!

Let's close our eyes and think about the wind, Pam said. Think of the windiest day you can remember.

Okay, Sam said. Sam remembered a storm that was so windy, a tree in front of his house blew over. He closed his eyes and thought about that very windy day.

Pretty soon, the sky started to get dark. It was getting windy.

Pam shouted, Hooray! Now we can go sailing.

Just then it got more windy and it started to rain. The wind even blew Pam's copies of Sail Away magazine out of the boat. Both Pam and Sam knew it was too dangerous to sail in this weather.

Gee, Sam, Pam said. You didn't have to think that hard!

ON YOUR OWN

You can make a snack that looks like a sailboat. Spread peanut butter inside a celery stick to make your boat. Then make a sail by cutting a triangle out of a fruit roll snack. Wrap your sail around a toothpick and stick the toothpick into the celery boat.

Order the numbers on the clothes below from smallest to largest to fit into the number line.

ON YOUR OWN

You can make your own number line game. Cut out several squares of paper and write a number on each piece. Use positive and negative numbers, fractions, decimals, and mixed numbers. Mix up the pieces and then put them back in order!

FACTOR FISHING

Factors of a number are those that divide evenly into the number.
Prime factors are numbers that are both factors and prime numbers.
Write the factors for each number. Then circle all of the factors that are prime factors.

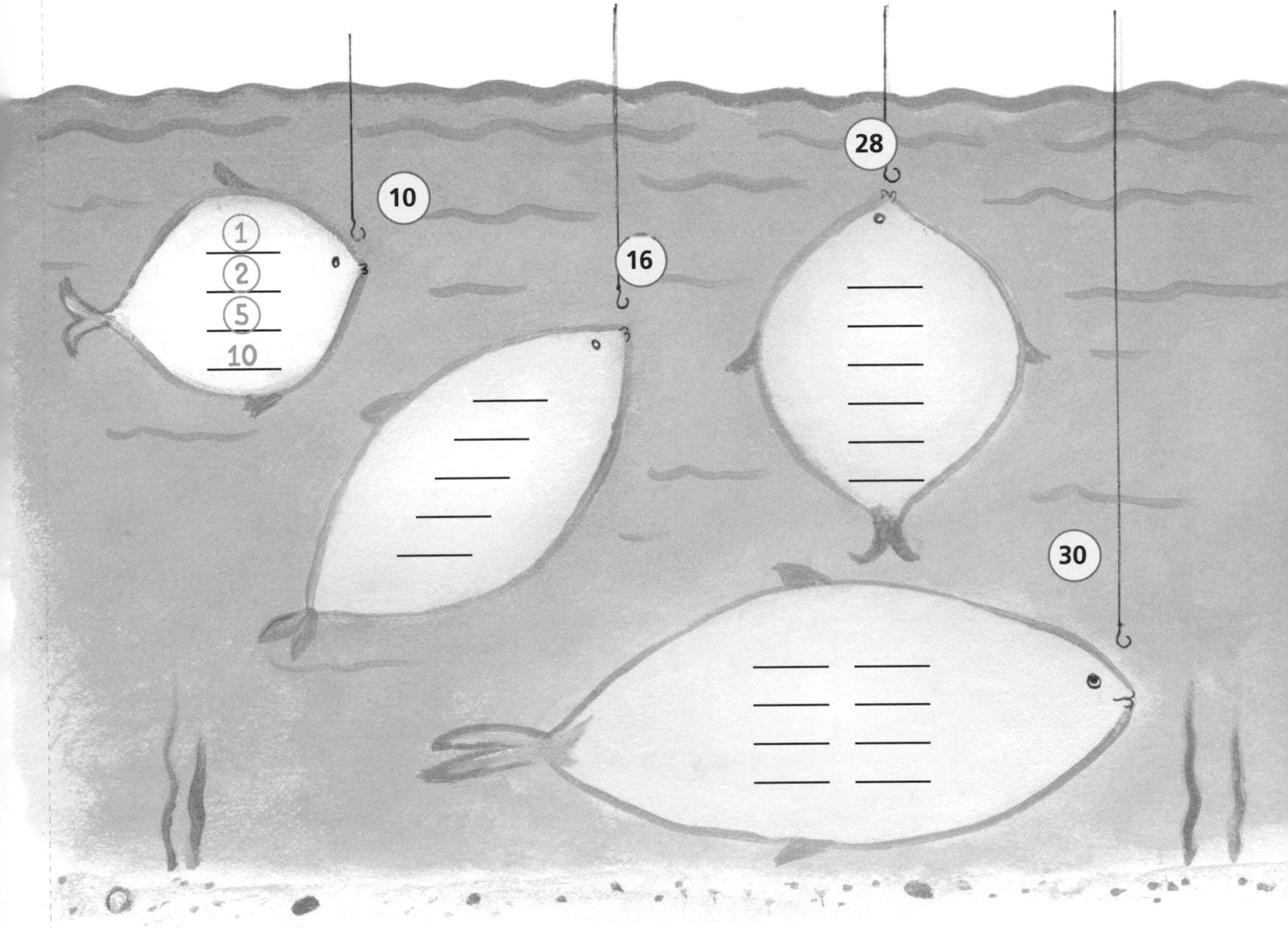

10

(1)
(2)
(5)
10

16

28

30

FAST FACT
Fishing has been around almost as long as fish have! In ancient times, people used bones for fishing hooks and vines for fishing lines.

THE CROSSING OF COLUMBUS

There are four false statements about Columbus in the boxes below. Cross out each box that has a false statement. Look at an encyclopedia if you need help.

1. King Ferdinand and Queen Isabella of Spain funded Columbus's voyage.	**2.** Columbus, like most people of his time, believed that the world was flat.	**3.** On his return voyage to Spain, Columbus brought back some of his discoveries, including pineapple, tobacco, and Native Americans.
4. On his first voyage, Columbus wanted to find a shortcut to India by sailing west instead of east.	**5.** The ships of his first voyage were named the *Nina*, *Pinta*, and *Santa Maria*.	**6.** Even up to his death, Columbus believed that he had reached Asia and India on his voyages.
7. Women were not allowed on any of Columbus's voyages.	**8.** Columbus believed that the ships of his first voyage had brought him good luck, so he used the same ships for all four of his voyages.	**9.** Columbus was the first European to explore North America and the United States.

FAST FACT

It took Columbus many years to convince someone to fund his voyage. He first proposed the idea to the court of Portugal, but they rejected it. He then spent seven years proposing his voyage to the court in Spain.

SCRAMBLED SYSTEMS

Unscramble the letters to name each system of the body.

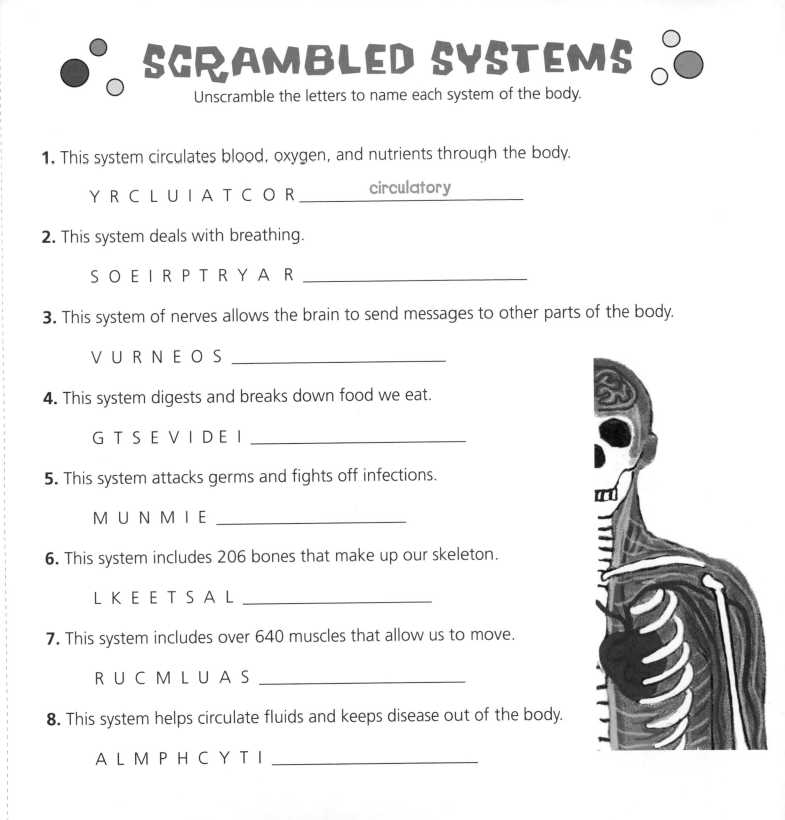

1. This system circulates blood, oxygen, and nutrients through the body.

Y R C L U I A T C O R _____circulatory_____

2. This system deals with breathing.

S O E I R P T R Y A R _____

3. This system of nerves allows the brain to send messages to other parts of the body.

V U R N E O S _____

4. This system digests and breaks down food we eat.

G T S E V I D E I _____

5. This system attacks germs and fights off infections.

M U N M I E _____

6. This system includes 206 bones that make up our skeleton.

L K E E T S A L _____

7. This system includes over 640 muscles that allow us to move.

R U C M L U A S _____

8. This system helps circulate fluids and keeps disease out of the body.

A L M P H C Y T I _____

ON YOUR OWN

Fill a glass with some water and add red food coloring. Then put a piece of celery in the water. After several minutes, the stalk will begin turning red. The red water is circulating through the celery, just as blood circulates through veins in your body!

CAMPING CONFLICT

Robin and Katie were so excited when their parents announced that the family was going on a summer camping trip. Both sisters loved being outdoors.

"All we need to do is decide what kind of campsite we want to go to, and then we can start planning," their dad said.

"Let's go camping by a lake," said Robin. "I really want to go swimming!"

"We can swim at the pool any time," said Katie. "Let's camp in the desert where I can go rock climbing."

"No way," said Robin. "The desert is too hot, and I don't know how to rock climb."

The sisters were angry with each other and they couldn't agree on a place for the family to camp. They argued all through dinner. Then their mom had an idea.

"Why don't we go camping at the beach?" she suggested. "Robin, you can swim in the ocean water. There are lots of rocks by the tide pools that Katie can explore."

"I don't know if I'd like swimming in salt water," said Robin.

"Rock climbing by the beach isn't the same as in the desert," Katie pointed out.

"It may not be exactly what you had in mind," Dad said, "but the beach is a good compromise. Both of you get to do what you want."

The girls finally agreed to go camping at the beach. Robin found that she enjoyed swimming in the ocean even more than in a lake. Katie had a great time climbing all the rocks by the water. Plus, the sisters discovered something that they both enjoyed equally. They liked building sand castles!

The **conflict** of a story is the main problem. The solution to that problem is called the **resolution**. Describe the conflict and the resolution of the story on the lines below.

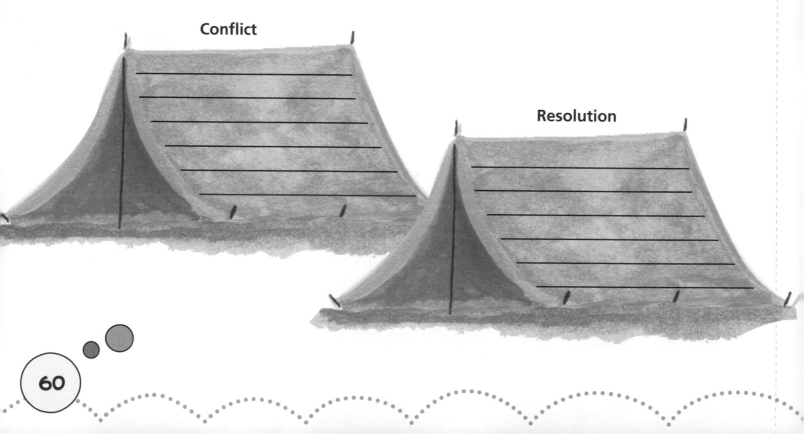

Conflict

Resolution

PICTURE THIS

A **fact** is something that we know for sure.
An **inference** is an educated guess based on clues.

Look at the picture below. Check off whether each statement is a fact or an inference about what you see in the picture.

The boy has scratches on his knee is a fact. We can see the scratches in the picture.

The boy is feeling a lot of pain is an inference. Based on his facial expression and the scratches on his knee, we can guess that he is in pain.

Read each statement and check off whether it is a fact about the picture or an inference.

	Fact	Inference
1. The boy hurt his knee.	✔	
2. The boy fell off his skateboard.		
3. The woman is bandaging the boy's knee.		
4. The woman is the boy's mother.		
5. The helmet is rolling away.		
6. It is raining outside.		
7. The boy was riding his skateboard too fast.		
8. The wet pavement caused the boy to fall off his skateboard.		
9. The skateboard is damaged.		
10. The boy feels upset about falling down.		

ON YOUR OWN

Find a picture in a magazine and make a list of all the facts and details you see in the picture. Then write some inferences that you can make based on those facts.

This number line shows both positive and negative numbers. The farther right you go on the number line, the greater the number is.

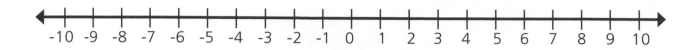

-10 -9 -8 -7 -6 -5 -4 -3 -2 -1 0 1 2 3 4 5 6 7 8 9 10

2 is greater than -6.
-1 is greater than -5.

Use the < or > symbol to show which number is greater in each pair. Then write the letters of the greater numbers in order on the lines below to complete the joke.

1. 2 < 9
G   A

2. -1 ◯ 3
Z   S

3. 5 ◯ -5
U   F

4. 3 ◯ -7
B   R

5. -4 ◯ -2
E   Z

6. 0 ◯ -3
E   S

7. -9 ◯ -1
N   R

8. 5 ◯ 0
O   T

What kind of sandwich did the negative number order?

____ _____ sandwich.

ON YOUR OWN

Get twenty-one index cards and write a number on each card. (Start at -10 and go up to 10. Don't forget zero!) Shuffle the cards and divide them between you and another player. Both players turn over a card, and whoever has the greater number keeps the cards. Keep playing until one player has all the cards!

ADD IT UP

You can add negative numbers together.
If both numbers are negative, just add the numbers together and keep the negative sign.

$$2 + 2 = 4 \qquad\qquad -2 + -2 = -4$$

Solve the problems by adding two negative numbers together.

1. The elevator went down one floor. Then it went down two more floors.
How many floors down is it now?
$\underline{\ -1 + -2 = -3\ }$

2. The elevator was 2 floors below the ground. It went down 3 more floors.
$-2 + -3 = \underline{\qquad}$

3. The elevator went down 5 floors. Then it went down 1 more floor.
$-5 + -1 = \underline{\qquad}$

4. The elevator started out 3 floors below the ground. Then it went down 6 more floors.
$-3 + \underline{\quad} = \underline{\qquad}$

5. The elevator went down 4 floors. Then it went down 4 more floors.
$\underline{\quad} + \underline{\quad} = \underline{\quad}$

6. $-6 + -2 = \underline{\qquad}$

7. $-5 + -4 = \underline{\qquad}$

8. $-8 + -1 = \underline{\qquad}$

9. $-3 + -4 = \underline{\qquad}$

10. $-2 + -9 = \underline{\qquad}$

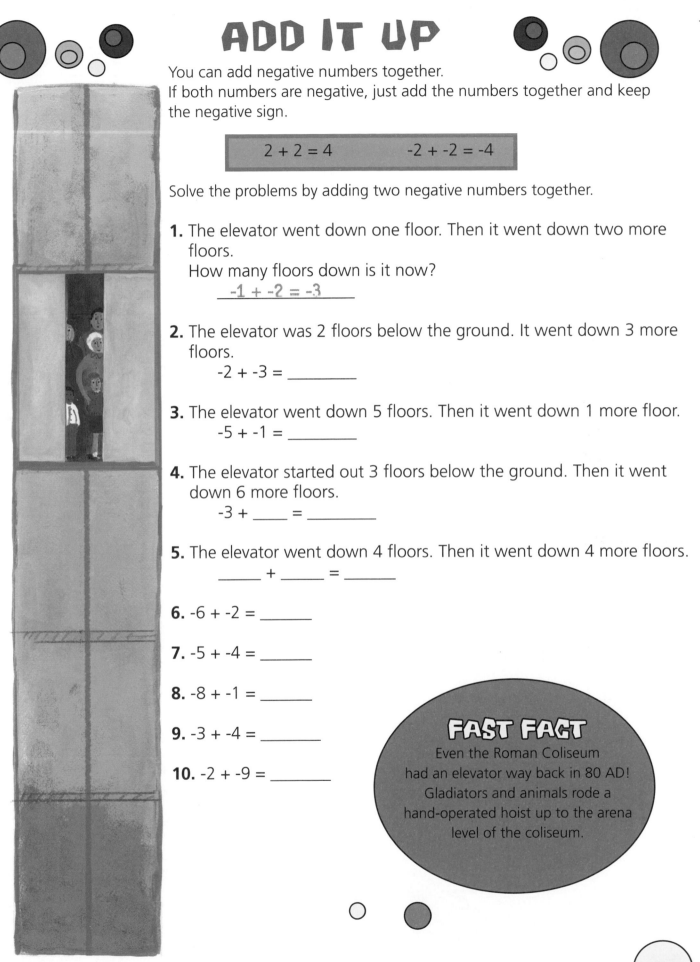

FAST FACT
Even the Roman Coliseum had an elevator way back in 80 AD! Gladiators and animals rode a hand-operated hoist up to the arena level of the coliseum.

CHIEF JOHN ROSS

One of the most important Native American leaders in American history didn't look like a Native American at all. His name was John Ross, and he had Cherokee ancestors that made him an eighth Cherokee. He helped fight for the rights of the Cherokee. In 1817, Ross was elected to the Cherokee National Council. He became the president of the council from 1819 to 1826.

Ross fought for the Cherokee with words instead of weapons. He wrote a constitution for the Cherokee people and was elected principal chief in 1828. They became the first Indian Republic. Ross's hope was that a star would be added to the U.S. flag to represent the Cherokee Nation.

Despite Ross's efforts, the Cherokee were still forced off their land. In 1838, John Ross had to lead his people from Georgia to Oklahoma. Thousands died on this journey, and it became known as the Trail of Tears. Even John Ross's wife died on the trek.

Once in Oklahoma, John Ross continued to serve as principal chief of the Cherokee Nation until his death. He died in Washington, D.C., where he had been working on a treaty between the Cherokee and the U.S. government.

Use context clues to connect each word with its meaning.

1. ancestor
2. elect
3. council
4. republic
5. treaty

a) to choose someone to be a leader
b) an agreement between two parties
c) a nation where the people elect their leaders
d) family relatives that lived in the past
e) a group of leaders that work together

6. Number the events to put them in the correct sequence.

_____ John Ross served as principal chief in Oklahoma.

_____ When the Cherokee were forced off their land, Ross led them from Georgia to Oklahoma on the Trail of Tears.

_____ John Ross served on the Cherokee National Council and became president.

_____ The Cherokee became the first Indian Republic and John Ross was elected the principal chief.

_____ In Washington, D.C., John Ross worked on a treaty between the Cherokee and the U.S. government.

FAST FACT
The Cherokee have their own language, which was invented by a Cherokee scholar named Sequoyah. Over 20,000 Cherokee people still speak this language today.

FOOD FACTORIES

Use the diagram to fill in the blanks below.

Photosynthesis

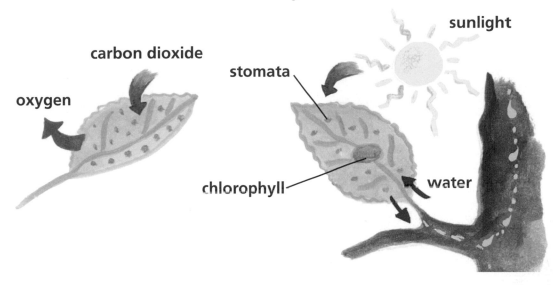

Plants are **Producers!**

Imagine if you could make your own food just by soaking up the sunlight. Plants can actually do this! They produce their own food, which is why we call them 1) ___producers___. The process of turning sunlight into food is called 2) _____. In fact, photosynthesis actually means "putting together by light."

     How do plants put together their own food? Leaves are the food factories of a plant. Leaves absorb 3) _____ and 4) _____. The roots of a plant suck up 5) _____ and deliver it to the leaves. The leaves then turn the water and carbon dioxide into sugar and starch.

     Producing food is a lot of work, and plants need energy to do it. Inside each leaf are green cells called 6) _____. These green cells trap the sunlight and use it as energy. With all this energy, plants actually make more food than they need. This extra food is 7) _____ that gets released back into the air. Tiny holes called 8) _____ are used for taking in the carbon dioxide and breathing out the oxygen.

     So, leaves are not only food factories for plants and trees, they give us air to breathe as well!

ON YOUR OWN

You can use leaves to create a piece of art. Put a leaf on a hard surface and cover it with a blank piece of paper. Then use a pencil to shade the area over the leaf. What do you see?

READING ROAD TRIP

Figure out the part of speech for each bold word. Write the word under the correct heading below.

Noun: a person, place, or thing
  sister, kitchen, chair
Proper noun: a person, place, or thing with a specific name.
  Susan, Disneyland, Rocky Mountains
  (Hint: Proper nouns always begin with capital letters.)
Verb: an action word.
  is, go, visit
Verb phrase: two or more words working together to express the action.
  should be, will go, can visit

Reggie Roberts was not excited about the two-week road trip his family had planned for the **summer**.

"We **should go** to Hawaii instead," said Reggie.

"I promise you **will have** a good time," his mom said.

The Roberts family left their home in Denver, **Colorado** and drove for two days until they **reached** Yellowstone National Park in Wyoming. They camped inside the park and visited a **geyser** named Old Faithful. **Reggie** was amazed as he watched tons of water shoot up out of a hole in the ground.

After staying at **Yellowstone** for a few days, they **packed** up their car again. They had to drive for three days to reach the Black Hills of South Dakota. Reggie's family visited a place called **Mount Rushmore**. Reggie **could hardly believe** that the faces of four **presidents** are actually carved into rock! A tour guide **told** him that each face is over 60 feet high and the whole monument took fourteen years to carve.

It **took** three more days for the family to drive back to Colorado. Reggie passed the time by reading some books he **had bought** about Mount Rushmore and watching the scenery. He was glad they had gone on the trip.

"It was a long **drive**," he said, "but it was worth it!"

Noun	Proper Noun	Verb	Verb Phrase
_____	_____	_____	_____
_____	_____	_____	_____
_____	_____	_____	_____
_____	_____	_____	_____

FAST FACT
Old Faithful is a geyser in Yellowstone Park. It shoots 8,400 gallons of boiling water 150 feet into the air. It does this about every 74 minutes, all day long!

DARE TO DESCRIBE

Adjectives and action words help make details come alive.
On the log ride, water went into our log and got us wet.
*On the log ride, **cold** water **splashed** into our log and **soaked** us!*

Rewrite each sentence to make it more descriptive. You can add adjectives, change verbs, or revise the whole sentence.

1. We rode on the roller coaster and went down a hill.

_____

2. We watched floats go by in the parade.

_____

3. The animal show had birds and monkeys.

_____

4. We rode on the bumper cars.

_____

5. My sister didn't want to go on the haunted house ride.

_____

6. We stopped to buy lemonade and take a rest.

_____

7. The Ferris wheel went fast and I got sick.

_____

8. At the arcade my sister won a prize.

_____

ON YOUR OWN
Think of the most exciting thing
you've done this summer and write
a list of words that describe it.
Then use those words to write a
descriptive paragraph.

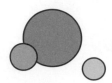

AVERAGE AVENUE

There are three kinds of averages: the **mode**, the **median**, and the **mean**.

> The **mode** is the number that occurs most often.
> 2, **5**, 3, 8, **5**, 2, **5**
>
> The mode is 5.

Find the mode in each set of numbers.

1. 14, 7, 3, 14, 12, 7, 14 _____

2. 45, 26, 28, 32, 26, 32, 26 _____

3. 3, -2, 1, -2, -1, -3 _____

> The **median** is the middle number in an ordered list of numbers.
> 4, 7, 12, 5, 8
> First, order the numbers from least to greatest.
> 4, 5, **7**, 8, 12
>
> The median is 7.

Find the median in each set of numbers.

4. 12, 5, 7, 10, 13 _____

5. 3, 15, 2, 9, 6, 11, 12 _____

6. -3, 2, 1, -2, 4 _____

> To find the **mean**, add all the numbers together.
> Then divide that sum by the total number of addends.
> 3, 9, 4, 3, 6
> 3 + 9 + 4 + 3 + 6 = 25
> There are 5 addends in the list. 25 divided by 5 = 5.
> The mean is 5.

Find the mean for each list of numbers.

7. 5, 1, 4, 2 _____

8. 7, 8, 5, 4 _____

9. 2, 4, 6, 1, 2 _____

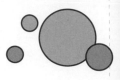

ON YOUR OWN
Write down the ages of everyone in your family. Then figure out the mode, the median, and the mean of the ages.

BARBEQUE BESTS

Circle the best unit for measuring each object.

1. The length of a [hot dog]   (inches)   foot   miles

2. The height of a [slide]   inches   feet   miles

3. The distance to the [sun]   inches   feet   miles

4. The length of an [ant]   centimeters   meters   kilometers

Circle the best weight estimate for each object.

5. [soda can]   16 ounces   16 pounds   16 tons

6. [picnic table]   200 ounces   200 pounds   200 tons

7. [ice]   30 ounces   30 pounds   30 tons

8. [truck]   2 ounces   2 pounds   2 tons

FAST FACT

Before there were rulers and measuring tapes, people actually used their own feet to measure things! This is why we use feet as a unit of measure today, although now it is a standard 12 inches.

KEY TO THE COLONIES

The original thirteen colonies can be divided into three regions. Each region used its natural resources to build its economy. Use the map and the key to list what each region did or produced.

New England: Massachusetts, New Hampshire, Rhode Island, Connecticut

ship building

_____

_____

_____

_____

Middle Colonies: New York, Delaware, New Jersey, Pennsylvania

_____

_____

_____

Southern Colonies: Virginia, Maryland, Georgia, North Carolina, South Carolina

_____

_____

_____

Key

🔨 **Factories**		🍚 **Rice**
🐟 **Fishing**		⛵ **Ship Building**
🌲 **Lumber**		🍃 **Tobacco**
🏭 **Mills**		🌾 **Wheat**

FAST FACT

Plymouth was actually not the first colony in America. Thirteen years before the pilgrims arrived, a colony named Jamestown was set up in Virginia.

SEARCH FOR THE SOURCE

Seventy-five percent of Earth's surface is covered in water. Over 97 percent of this water is in the ocean. Only about 3 percent of Earth's surface is freshwater, or water that is not in the ocean.

Water Source	Percentage of Total Water
Oceans	97.24%
Ice Caps, Glaciers	2.14%
Groundwater	.61%
Freshwater Lakes	.009%
Inland Seas	.008%
Soil Moisture	.005%
Atmosphere	.001%
Rivers	.0001%

FAST FACT

Even though rivers make up only .0001% of Earth's total water, they are the source for most of the water we use every day.

Find each of the water sources in the word search below.

```
F  R  E  S  H  W  A  T  E  R  L  A  K  E  S
R  I  L  S  H  S  O  I  O  M  O  T  F  R  O
O  V  A  R  I  V  L  K  C  R  S  M  O  C  I
C  E  K  G  O  C  A  R  E  F  G  O  N  D  L
A  I  N  L  A  N  D  S  E  A  S  S  G  H  M
N  C  I  A  S  O  L  I  N  L  A  P  N  D  O
W  E  L  C  G  R  O  U  S  O  L  H  M  O  I
T  C  A  I  W  A  T  R  I  V  G  E  G  L  S
R  A  N  E  I  C  A  P  S  G  L  R  K  E  T
A  P  S  R  I  V  E  R  S  R  L  E  K  E  U
T  S  E  S  G  R  O  U  N  D  W  A  T  E  R
M  G  A  S  I  N  L  O  C  E  A  N  S  V  E
```

A WHALE TALE

Read the paragraph. Then complete the graphic organizer.

There are over 75 different types of whales swimming in our ocean. Some weigh in at 150 tons, and others are just a few feet long. But all whales, no matter how big or small, can be classified into two groups: toothed whales and baleen whales.

Toothed whales have sharp teeth for eating fish and plants. Dolphins and porpoises are actually types of toothed whales. The killer whale is another type of toothed whale.

Baleen whales do not have any teeth. They have plates attached to their jawbones. Baleen whales simply open their mouths and suck in seawater. The plates filter out plankton and krill for the whale to eat. Baleen whales are sometimes called filter feeders. Some types of baleen whales include blue whales, humpback whales, and gray whales.

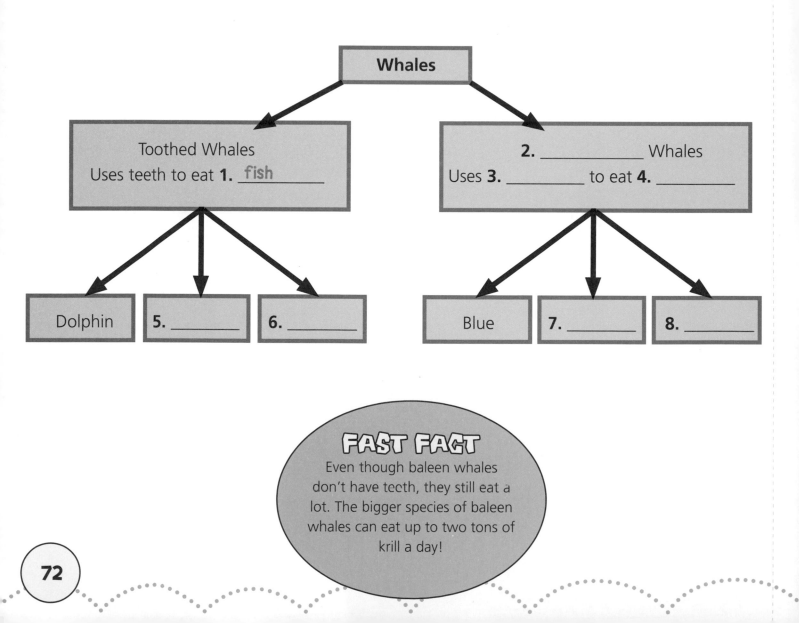

Whales

Toothed Whales
Uses teeth to eat **1.** _fish_

2. _____ Whales
Uses **3.** _____ to eat **4.** _____

Dolphin **5.** _____ **6.** _____

Blue **7.** _____ **8.** _____

FAST FACT
Even though baleen whales don't have teeth, they still eat a lot. The bigger species of baleen whales can eat up to two tons of krill a day!

72

A word that ends in **ing** can be part of a **verb** or it can be a noun.
A noun that ends in **ing** is called a **gerund**.

Verbs: I *went skating*.
Let's *go walking*.
Gerunds: *Skating* on the ice is fun.
I like *walking* in the woods.

Figure out if the underlined word in each sentence is a verb or a gerund, then circle the correct term for each.

1. Most campers went <u>hiking</u> in the hills every day.	(Verb)	Gerund
2. <u>Fishing</u> was a fun way to spend the afternoon.	Verb	Gerund
3. Campers said that <u>swimming</u> was their favorite activity.	Verb	Gerund
4. The older campers went <u>biking</u> on mountain trails.	Verb	Gerund
5. <u>Boating</u> on the lake was not allowed when it was raining.	Verb	Gerund
6. Every night the campers were <u>singing</u> around the campfire.	Verb	Gerund
7. All the campers helped with the <u>cleaning</u> after dinner.	Verb	Gerund
8. Campers could take lessons to improve their horseback <u>riding</u>.	Verb	Gerund

ON YOUR OWN

Make a list of all the activities you would enjoy doing at summer camp. Then count how many gerunds are in your list.

TYPES OF TRIANGLES

Look at the types of triangles.
Then label each triangle below.

An **equilateral triangle** has all congruent sides.

An **isosceles triangle** has two congruent sides.

A **scalene triangle** has no congruent sides.

A **right triangle** has one right angle.

1.
_____equilateral_____

2.
_____

3.
_____

4.
_____

5.
_____

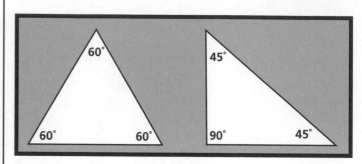

The angles of a triangle always add up to 180.

Figure out the number of degrees in the third angle of each triangle.

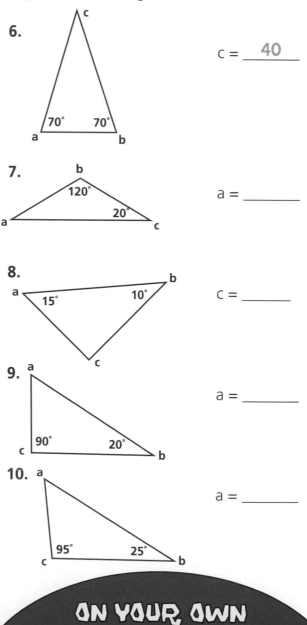

6.
c = ___40___

7.
a = _____

8.
c = _____

9.
a = _____

10.
a = _____

ON YOUR OWN
Find all the triangle shaped objects you can in your own home. Decide if each triangle is equilateral, isosceles, or scalene.

A **quadrilateral** is a four-sided shape. The angles in a quadrilateral always add up to 360 degrees.

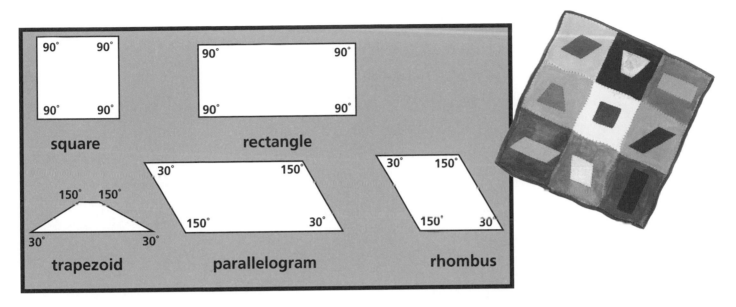

90° 90° / 90° 90° **square**	90° 90° / 90° 90° **rectangle**
150° 150° / 30° 30° **trapezoid**	30° 150° / 150° 30° **parallelogram**
	30° 150° / 150° 30° **rhombus**

Label each shape and figure out the number of degrees in the fourth angle. Remember, the angles will all add up to 360.

1.
A 90°   90° B
90° C
D

square
D = __90°__

2.
A 45°   135° B
C   45° D

C = _____

3.
D C
155°
25°   25°
A   B

D = _____

4.
A
15° B
165°
D 15°
C

D = _____

5.
A 120° B
60° 120°
D C

B = _____

6.
A   140° B
140°   40°
D C

A = _____

7.
A   90° B
90°   90°
D   C

A = _____

8.
A 90° B
90° 90°
D   C

B = _____

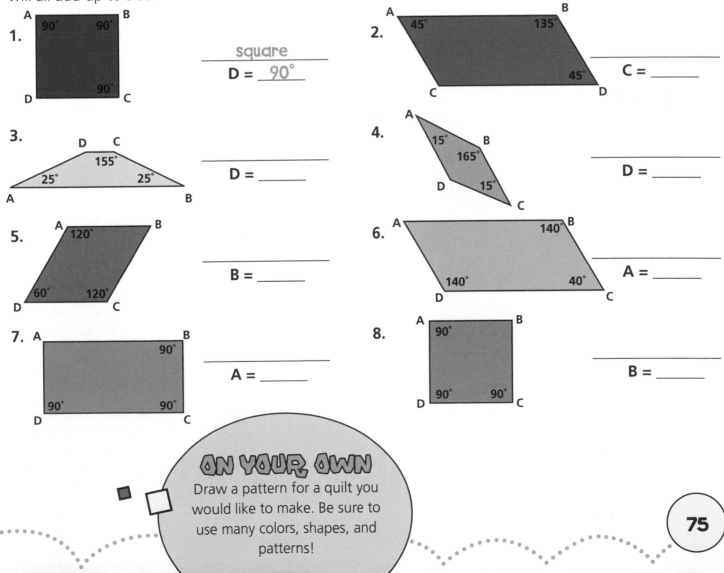

ON YOUR OWN
Draw a pattern for a quilt you would like to make. Be sure to use many colors, shapes, and patterns!

PORTRAIT OF A HERO

On a hot summer day in 1778, General Washington's army battled against the British near Monmouth, New Jersey. In the midst of flying bullets, a woman named Mary Hays McCauly was busy helping the soldiers. The men called her Molly Pitcher because she brought pitchers of cool water to tired, thirsty solders on the field.

Molly's husband, William Hays, was one of the soldiers in the battle. When he fell wounded, Molly quickly took his place and manned the cannon. Even during heavy enemy fire, Molly stayed behind the cannon and fired back. She also helped take care of the wounded soldiers. One time, she carried a wounded soldier off the battlefield to safety.

For her heroic actions, General Washington made her a noncommissioned officer. After this, she was known as Sergeant Molly. If you visit the battle site, you'll see a sculpture of Sergeant Molly on the battle monument.

Write some words that describe the qualities of a hero.

brave

What actions show that Molly Pitcher is a hero?

_____
_____
_____
_____
_____
_____

FAST FACT

Molly Pitcher has an award named after her! Every year the Molly Pitcher Award is given to someone who voluntarily contributes to the armed forces.

WEATHER WATCH

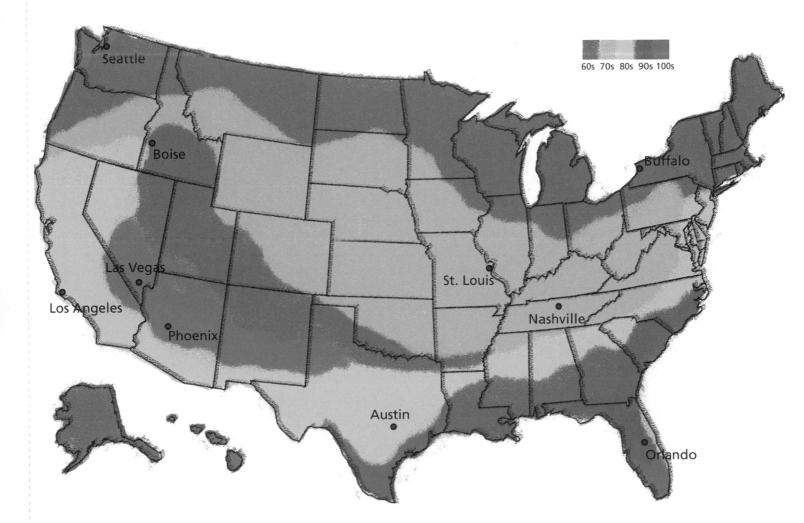

60s 70s 80s 90s 100s

Refer to the map and list the cities for each temperature range.

1. 60s _____Buffalo_____, _____Seattle_____

2. 70s _____, _____

3. 80s _____, _____

4. 90s _____, _____

5. 100s _____, _____

ON YOUR OWN
Look at the weather map in your local newspaper and predict the weather for the next five days. Then keep a log of the weather and see if your forecast was correct!

PROOFREADING PALS

Kevin wrote a letter to his pen pal, but his letter has mistakes and sentences that need to be combined. Fix the problems in Kevin's letter and rewrite it. If the sentence has the [cube icon], there is an error that needs to be corrected. If you see the [pencil icon], the sentence should be combined.

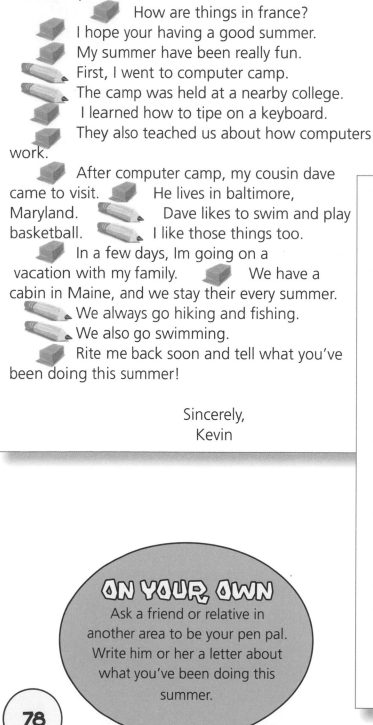

Dear Phillip,

How are things in france?

I hope your having a good summer.

My summer have been really fun.

First, I went to computer camp.

The camp was held at a nearby college.

I learned how to tipe on a keyboard.

They also teached us about how computers work.

After computer camp, my cousin dave came to visit. He lives in baltimore, Maryland. Dave likes to swim and play basketball. I like those things too.

In a few days, Im going on a vacation with my family. We have a cabin in Maine, and we stay their every summer.

We always go hiking and fishing.

We also go swimming.

Rite me back soon and tell what you've been doing this summer!

Sincerely,
Kevin

ON YOUR OWN

Ask a friend or relative in another area to be your pen pal. Write him or her a letter about what you've been doing this summer.

Dear Phillip,

_____

_____

_____

_____

_____

_____

_____

_____

_____

_____

_____

_____

_____

_____

_____

_____

_____

_____

Sincerely,
Kevin

SUE'S CLUES

A **conclusion** is when you use clues to find out something that is not directly stated.

Read each set of clues and circle the best conclusion.

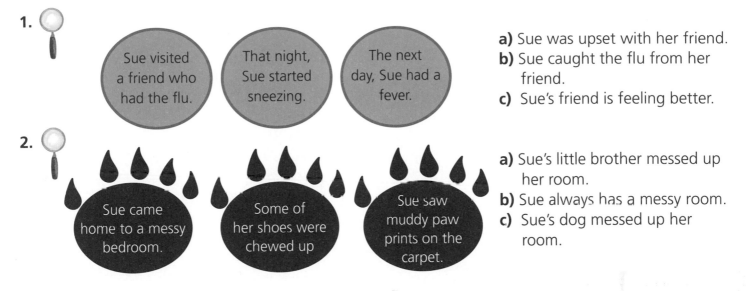

1.

Sue visited a friend who had the flu.

That night, Sue started sneezing.

The next day, Sue had a fever.

a) Sue was upset with her friend.
b) Sue caught the flu from her friend.
c) Sue's friend is feeling better.

2.

Sue came home to a messy bedroom.

Some of her shoes were chewed up

Sue saw muddy paw prints on the carpet.

a) Sue's little brother messed up her room.
b) Sue always has a messy room.
c) Sue's dog messed up her room.

Read the story. Look for the clues that led to Sue's conclusion and write them on the lines below.

Whenever Sue made cookies, she always brought some to her next-door-neighbor Mrs. Taylor. One night, Sue took some cookies over to Mrs. Taylor's house and rang the doorbell. Nobody was home. The house was very dark.

Sue decided that she would leave the cookies in Mrs. Taylor's mailbox. But there was no room because the mailbox was full of mail! Nobody had gotten the mail for a few days. Sue also noticed that a few newspapers were stacked on Mrs. Taylor's porch.

For the next few days, Sue watched Mrs. Taylor's house. She didn't see Mrs. Taylor come home. Sue concluded that Mrs. Taylor must be on vacation. So, Sue ate all the cookies by herself!

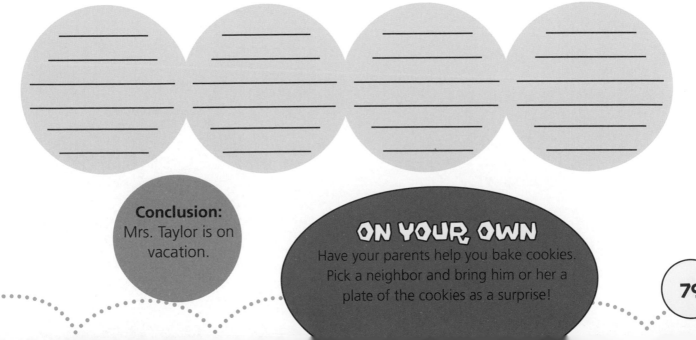

Conclusion: Mrs. Taylor is on vacation.

ON YOUR OWN
Have your parents help you bake cookies. Pick a neighbor and bring him or her a plate of the cookies as a surprise!

FRACTION ADD-VENTURE

To add two like fractions, add only the numerators.

$$\frac{2}{6} + \frac{1}{6} = \frac{3}{6} = \frac{1}{2}$$

$$\frac{2}{4} + \frac{3}{4} = \frac{5}{4} = 1\frac{1}{4}$$

Add the fractions. Show the answers in lowest terms.

1. $\frac{2}{10} + \frac{4}{10} = \frac{6}{10} = \frac{3}{5}$

2. $\frac{5}{8} + \frac{1}{8} = $ _____ = _____

3. $\frac{1}{2} + \frac{1}{2} = $ _____ = _____

4. $\frac{3}{5} + \frac{3}{5} = $ _____ = _____

5. $\frac{2}{7} + \frac{3}{7} = $ _____

6. $\frac{4}{8} + \frac{1}{8} = $ _____

7. $\frac{1}{12} + \frac{5}{12} = $ _____ = _____

8. $\frac{6}{11} + \frac{4}{11} = $ _____

9. $\frac{3}{6} + \frac{1}{6} = $ _____ = _____

10. $\frac{2}{3} + \frac{2}{3} = $ _____ = _____

FAST FACT

The word **cliffhanger** describes a movie that has an ending that leaves you hanging. But a cliffhanger is also a real tool that's used in rock climbing. It's a special hook that climbers use to help them get over a ledge.

HOW LOW CAN YOU GO?

Unlike fractions do not have the same denominator.
To add or subtract unlike fractions, you have to find the **least common denominator**, or the **LCD**.

$\frac{1}{6}$ and $\frac{1}{4}$ are unlike fractions.
The lowest number that can be divided by both 6 and 4 is 12.

$\frac{1}{6} = \frac{2}{12}$

$\frac{1}{4} = \frac{3}{12}$ The lowest common denominator of **6** and **4** is **12**.

Use the LCD to convert the unlike fractions to like fractions.

1. $\frac{1}{3}$, $\frac{1}{2}$ $\frac{2}{6}$, $\frac{3}{6}$

LCD 6

2. $\frac{2}{3}$, $\frac{1}{6}$ _____ , _____

LCD 6

3. $\frac{3}{5}$, $\frac{1}{3}$ _____ , _____

LCD 15

4. $\frac{4}{8}$, $\frac{3}{4}$ _____ , _____

LCD 8

Find the LCD for each pair of fractions.

5. $\frac{2}{4}$, $\frac{1}{3}$

LCD = _____

6. $\frac{5}{6}$, $\frac{4}{9}$

LCD = _____

7. $\frac{3}{10}$, $\frac{1}{4}$

LCD = _____

8. $\frac{2}{3}$, $\frac{8}{9}$

LCD = _____

ON YOUR OWN
Find out how low you can go! Have two friends hold onto the ends of a piece of string or yarn. Keep lowering the string until you can't go under it without falling.

WESTWARD WAYS

In the early 1800s' explorers set out to see the west. Meriwether Lewis and William Clark were one team that journeyed west. Zebulon Pike also went west but took a different route. Trace the two exploration routes.

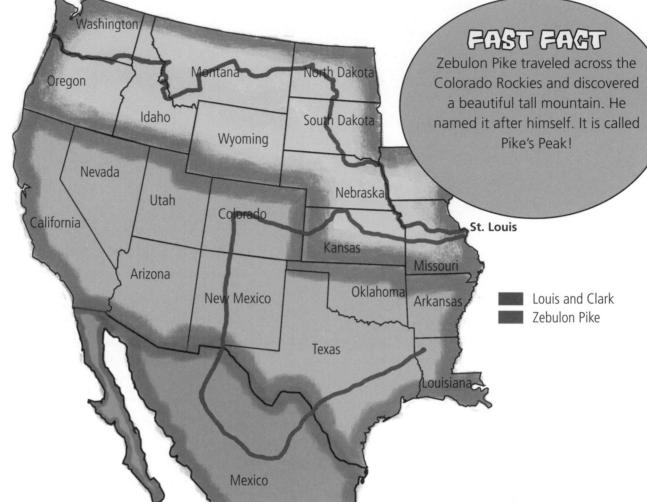

FAST FACT
Zebulon Pike traveled across the Colorado Rockies and discovered a beautiful tall mountain. He named it after himself. It is called Pike's Peak!

Louis and Clark
Zebulon Pike

Read each statement and check off the explorer who followed that route. If the statement is true for both routes, then check both columns.

	Pike	Lewis and Clark
1. Started in St. Louis	✔	✔
2. Started out following the Missouri River		
3. Started out following the Mississippi River		
4. Went all the way to the coast of the Pacific Ocean		
5. Went through the Rocky Mountains		
6. Went along the Rio Grande		
7. Passed the Snake River and the Columbia River		
8. Went as far south as Mexico		

A SUPER STAR

What gives us heat, light, warmth, and energy and is at the center of our solar system? The Sun! The Sun is actually a star, just like the other stars you see in the night sky. The Sun, like all stars, is made of gas. At the center, or core, of the Sun, hydrogen gas is turned into helium gas. This reaction gives off heat and light.

The Sun is very hot. On the surface it's about 6,000 degrees Celsius. The atmosphere around the surface is even hotter, with temperatures in the millions of degrees. Some spots on the Sun's surface appear darker because they are slightly cooler. These are called sunspots.

Most people think that stars are smaller than planets, but the Sun is much bigger than Earth. About 109 planets the size of Earth would fit across the diameter of the Sun. If the Sun were hollow, about a million Earths would fit inside. Practically everything on Earth depends on the Sun, including people, plants, and animals. It really is a super star!

1. What happens in the Sun's core? _Hydrogen gas is turned into helium gas._

2. How hot is the Sun? _____
_____.

3. What are sunspots? _____
_____.

4. How big is the Sun compared to Earth? _____
_____.

5. Why is the Sun important to us here on Earth? _____
_____.

ON YOUR OWN
Think about all the things that would happen if the Sun didn't shine. We wouldn't have any natural light, plants wouldn't grow, and we would all be very cold! Write a story about a day with no sunshine.

A REASON FOR THE SEASON

Persuasive writing gives an argument and supports it with reasons. Read each passage. Then summarize the author's argument and the reasons given to support it.

Summer Is Super

Summer is the best season of the year. First of all, warm summer weather is great. The Sun shines almost every day, so you can be outdoors all the time, even at night! Because of the warm weather, summer is perfect for swimming, hiking, or boating.

   Of course, the best thing about summer is that you have a vacation from school. You can relax, travel, and spend time with your friends and family. Summer offers more freedom and fun than any other season!

1. Argument: The best season in the year is _____.
2. Reasons: _____
_____
_____

Wonderful Winter

Winter is the best season because it has something to offer everyone. If you like to stay indoors, winter is perfect for curling up beside a fire. If you like to be outdoors, you can ski, snowboard, or sled in the winter snow. Bundling up in coats and scarves is always fun.

   Winter is very special because there are so many festive holidays to celebrate. Family and friends come together to share these special times. Winter is the perfect time to make special memories.

3. Argument: The best season in the year is _____.
4. Reasons: _____
_____
_____

5. Which argument do you agree with and why? _____
_____
_____

FAST FACT
Seasons are different depending on where you live in the world. Some places have only two seasons—a wet season and a dry season. December is a cool month for most places in the United States, but it's hot in Australia!

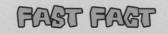

HOORAY FOR HOLIDAYS

Come up with a new holiday that you think should be added to the calendar. First, brainstorm some ideas about your holiday. What makes this holiday special? How would people celebrate it? Why should it be added to the calendar?

My New Holiday

_____

_____

_____

_____

_____

_____

_____

_____

_____

_____

_____

_____

_____

_____

On a separate piece of paper use your ideas to write a persuasive paragraph. Try to convince someone that your holiday should be celebrated. Include lots of reasons to support your point!

ON YOUR OWN

Think of something that should be changed in your neighborhood, and write a letter to your city mayor about it. Include lots of good reasons to support your idea. Mail your letter, and see if you get a letter back!

SHAPE UP

The **perimeter** of a shape is the sum of all the sides added together.
The **area of a quadrilateral** = length x height.
The **area of a triangle** = $\frac{1}{2}$ x length x height.

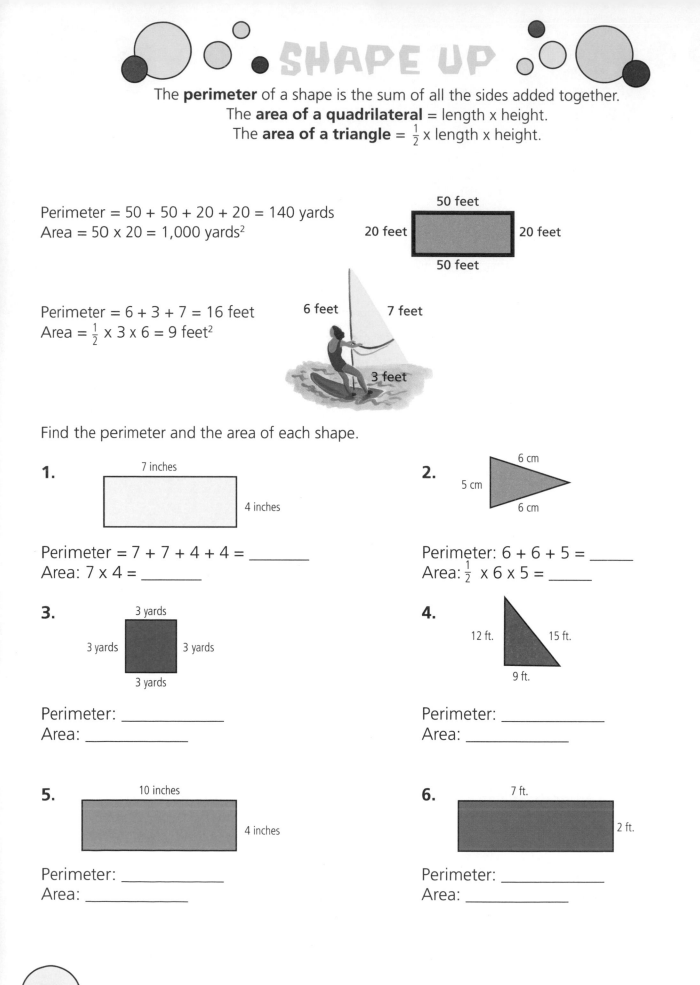

Perimeter = 50 + 50 + 20 + 20 = 140 yards
Area = 50 x 20 = 1,000 yards²

50 feet
20 feet   20 feet
50 feet

Perimeter = 6 + 3 + 7 = 16 feet
Area = $\frac{1}{2}$ x 3 x 6 = 9 feet²

6 feet   7 feet

3 feet

Find the perimeter and the area of each shape.

1.

7 inches

4 inches

Perimeter = 7 + 7 + 4 + 4 = _____
Area: 7 x 4 = _____

2.

6 cm

5 cm

6 cm

Perimeter: 6 + 6 + 5 = _____
Area: $\frac{1}{2}$ x 6 x 5 = _____

3.

3 yards

3 yards   3 yards

3 yards

Perimeter: _____
Area: _____

4.

12 ft.   15 ft.

9 ft.

Perimeter: _____
Area: _____

5.

10 inches

4 inches

Perimeter: _____
Area: _____

6.

7 ft.

2 ft.

Perimeter: _____
Area: _____

TURN UP THE VOLUME

The **volume** is the number of cubic units that fit inside a figure.
To find the volume, multiply the length, the width, and the height.

$$v = l \times w \times h$$

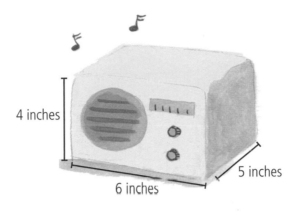

volume = 6 x 5 x 4 = 120 inches³

Find the volume of each.

1.

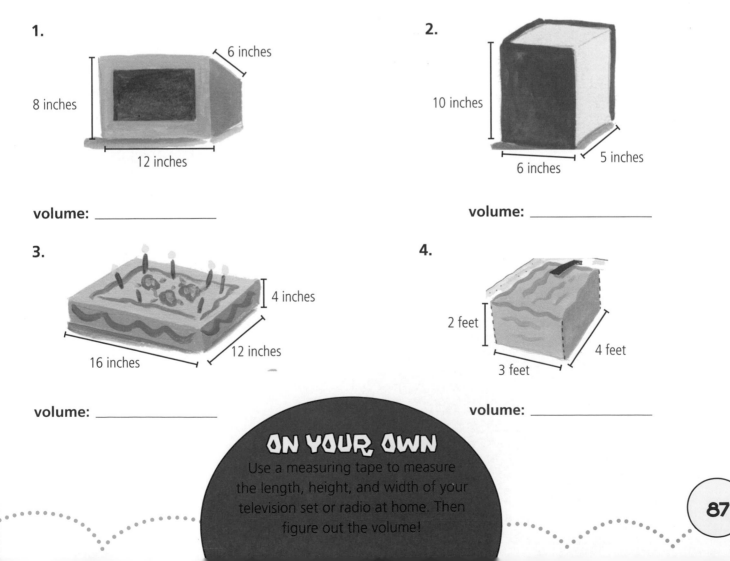

6 inches

8 inches

12 inches

volume: _____

2.

10 inches

6 inches

5 inches

volume: _____

3.

4 inches

16 inches

12 inches

volume: _____

4.

2 feet

3 feet

4 feet

volume: _____

ON YOUR OWN

Use a measuring tape to measure the length, height, and width of your television set or radio at home. Then figure out the volume!

87

Find each state on the map and write the capital city.

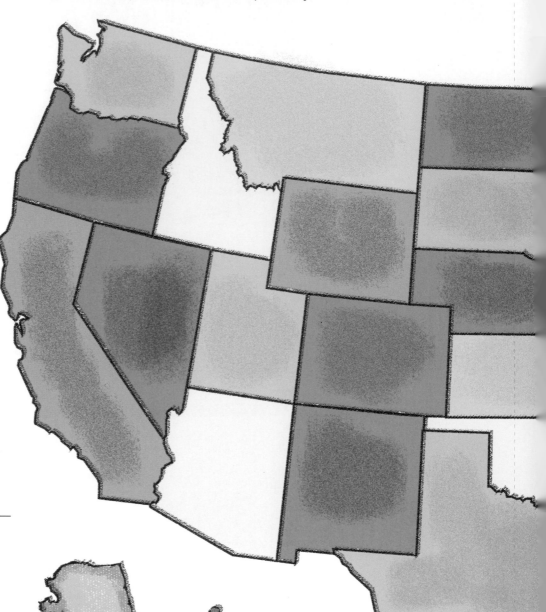

Alabama: _____

Alaska: _____

Arizona: _____

Arkansas: _____

California: _____

Colorado: _____

Connecticut: _____

Delaware: _____

Florida: _____

Georgia: _____

Hawaii: _____

Idaho: _____

Illinois: _____

Indiana: _____

Iowa: _____

Kansas: _____

Kentucky: _____

Louisiana: _____

Maine: _____

Maryland: _____

Massachusetts: _____

Michigan: _____

Minnesota: _____

Mississippi: _____

Missouri: _____

FAST FACT

Washington, D.C., the capital of the United States, is actually named after two important men. The first word, Washington, is named after George Washington. The second part, D.C., is short for the District of Columbia, which honors Christopher Columbus.

Montana: _____
Nebraska: _____
Nevada: _____
New Hampshire: _____
New Jersey: _____
New Mexico: _____
New York: _____
North Carolina: _____
North Dakota: _____
Ohio: _____
Oklahoma: _____
Oregon: _____
Pennsylvania: _____
Rhode Island: _____
South Carolina: _____
South Dakota: _____
Tennessee: _____
Texas: _____
Utah: _____
Vermont: _____
Virginia: _____
Washington: _____
West Virginia: _____
Wisconsin: _____
Wyoming: _____

ON YOUR OWN

Trace this map of the United States onto a separate piece of paper. Try to label all the states and capitals from memory!

BOOK REPORT

It's time to write your very own book report! First, choose a book that tells a story. After you read it, complete the sentences below.

Book Title: _____

Author: _____

This story is about _____.

The main characters are _____.

_____ is _____.

(character name)   (describe the character)

_____ is _____.

(a different character name)   (describe the character)

The story takes place in _____.

This mood of the story is _____.

The main conflict in the story is _____

_____.

The resolution happens when _____

_____.

The theme of the story is _____

_____.

I would / would not recommend this book to a friend because _____

_____

_____.

ON YOUR OWN

Ask your friends to make a list of their top five favorite books. Put all the books together on one list. Share the list with your friends, and read as many of the books as you can!

STATE REPORT

Look up your state in an encyclopedia. Fill in the blanks below with information about the state you live in. When you're done, you'll have a State Report!

State Name: _____

Population: _____

Capital City: _____

Largest City: _____

State Motto: _____

_____

State Bird: _____

State Flower: _____

Natural Features:

What kind of physical features does your state have? Are there mountain ranges, rivers, deserts, or lakes? Name some of these features and describe them.

_____
_____
_____
_____
_____
_____
_____

Climate:

What kind of weather does your state have? How much rainfall and snowfall does the state get in a year? What is the average temperature?

_____
_____
_____
_____
_____
_____

History:
How and when did your state become a state? Name a historic person or place in your state. _____
_____
_____
_____
_____
_____
_____
_____
_____

FAST FACT
Many states have added more symbols over the years. Some states have a state animal, state insect, state fish, state fruit, or state fossil. Some states even have a state dance and a state song!

SUMMER READING LIST

Here are some books for readers going into fifth grade to enjoy during the summer months.

My Brother Sam Is Dead by James L. Collier and Christopher Collier
The Revolutionary War is seen through the eyes of the Meeker family when one son joins the Rebel forces.

Walk Two Moons by Sharon Creech
In search of a mother who never returned, a thirteen-year-old girl travels west to Idaho with her grandparents.

The Watsons Go to Birmingham by Christopher Paul Curtis
When Byron and his family visit their grandmother in Birmingham, they get an up-close look at racial conflicts in 1963.

We the People by Bobbi Katz
Important people and events in American history are highlighted in 65 original poems.

The View from Saturday by E. L. Konigsburg
The stories of four students and their handicapped teacher are woven together as they prepare for an academic bowl.

Number the Stars by Lois Lowry
In Denmark in 1943, Annemarie's best friend, Ellen Rosen, finds refuge in Annemarie's home by pretending to be one of the family.

Sing Down the Moon by Scott O'Dell
This book tells the story of the Indians' forced removal and journey to Fort Sumner, as seen through the eyes of a young Navajo girl.

Bridge to Terabithia by Katherine Paterson
Jess and Leslie forge a bond of friendship as they create a fantasy world called Terabithia in the forest.

A Long Way from Chicago by Richard Peck
When Joey and his younger sister spend the summer with their grandmother in a small town, they learn that you don't have to be in the big city to have an adventure.

Hatchet by Gary Paulsen
Thirteen-year-old Brian Robeson survives a plane crash and must fend for himself in the Canadian wilderness with nothing but the clothes on his back and a hatchet his mother gave him.

Holes by Louis Sachar
After being falsely accused of stealing some sneakers, Stanley Yelnats is sentenced to a juvenile work camp in the desert.

The Sign of the Beaver by Elizabeth George Speare
Left alone to guard his family's frontier home, twelve-year-old Matt is befriended by a Native-American boy who helps him learn how to survive.

The Trouble with Tuck by Theodore Taylor
When Helen realizes that her beloved dog Tuck has gone blind, she trains him to follow a guide dog of his own.

Caleb's Choice by G. Clifton Wisler
Caleb must decide whether or not to help two runaway slaves escape to freedom.

SUMMER ACTIVITIES AND PROJECTS

Birdwatching
Birds will flock to your home if you set out a birdfeeder for them. Take a pine cone and spread peanut butter on it, then roll it in birdseed. Use a string to hang it outside, and watch the birds come to take a nibble.

Book Swap
Have a book swap with your friends. Ask each friend to bring a book and tell what it's about. Have everyone swap books with someone else.

A Cool Collection
Start a new collection! Pick something you can easily find outside, like leaves, seashells, or rocks. Find a special place to keep all the items in your collection.

Face-painting Fun
Make your own face paint by mixing 1 teaspoon of cornstarch with $\frac{1}{2}$ teaspoon of water and $\frac{1}{2}$ teaspoon of cold cream. Add food coloring to create different colors. Have fun painting faces with a friend!

An Interesting Interview
Interview a grandparent or another older person and find out what life was like when he or she was growing up. Record the interview on video or tape.

It's Story Time!
Use your imagination to turn pictures into a story. Pick four or five different pictures from a magazine. Then come up with a story to go along with the pictures. Switch the order of the pictures and make up a whole new story.

Making Music
You can make music with a few basic kitchen items. Get some glasses and fill each one with a different amount of water. Then use a teaspoon to tap the sides of the glasses. Each glass will chime a different sound, depending on how much water is in it.

Memory Box
Make a memory box by decorating an old shoebox with paper and markers. Use the box to keep photographs, cards, awards, and anything else that is special to you.

Mini-Golf at Home
Set up a miniature golf course in your own backyard. Use old boxes and cans to set up obstacles on each hole. You can use an old tennis ball in place of a golf ball and a wrapping paper tube for a golf club.

Timeline Project
Make a timeline of your life. Describe important events in your own life, starting with your birth. Add important events that happened in the world during your lifetime as well.

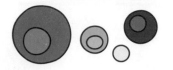 

Page 6
2. a
3. b
4. b
Answers to problems 5 and 6 will vary.

Page 7
2. He tripped and fell down.
3. Ralph forgot his homework.
4. Ralph sat on bubble gum.

Page 8
2. 5,531
3. 1,636
4. 6,025
5. 2,213
6. 6,949
7. 3,791
8. 5,842
9. 6,868
10. 8,555
11. 7,887
12. 3,953
13. 7,851
14. 8,585

Page 9
2. $6 + 4 = 10$
$4 + 6 = 10$
$10 - 4 = 6$
$10 - 6 = 4$
3. $5 \times 6 = 30$
$6 \times 5 = 30$
$30 \div 6 = 5$
$30 \div 5 = 6$
4. $7 \times 3 = 21$
$3 \times 7 = 21$
$21 \div 3 = 7$
$21 \div 7 = 3$
5. $8 + 6 = 14$
$6 + 8 = 14$
$14 - 6 = 8$
$14 - 8 = 6$
6. $5 \times 4 = 20$
$4 \times 5 = 20$
$20 \div 4 = 5$
$20 \div 5 = 4$
7. $9 \times 8 = 72$
$8 \times 9 = 72$
$72 \div 9 = 8$
$72 \div 8 = 9$
8. $5 + 6 = 11$
$6 + 5 = 11$
$11 - 6 = 5$
$11 - 5 = 6$
9. $8 \times 7 = 56$
$7 \times 8 = 56$
$56 \div 8 = 7$
$56 \div 7 = 8$

Page 10
Answers will vary.

Page 11
Answers to questions 2 and 3 will vary.
4. Leopard: predator
Baboon: prey
5. Giraffe: prey
Lion: predator
6. Lion: predator
Zebra: prey
7. Herbivores:
Zebra, Giraffe, Baboon
8. Carnivores:
Leopard, Lion

Page 12
2. f
3. e
4. g
5. d
6. h
7. a
8. b

Page 13
2. spear
3. spear
4. horse
5. horse
6. ax
7. ax
8. tree limb

Page 14
1. b) 579,000 c) 580,000
d) 600,000
2. a) 344,800 b) 345,000
c) 340,000 d) 300,000
3. a) 2,488,300
b) 2,488,000 c) 2,490,000
d) 2,500,000

Page 15
1. 5,843; 8,324; 54,388; 58,488
2. 6,279, 69,599; 675,922; 697,299

Page 16
2. e
3. b
4. a
5. h
6. c

7. g
8. f

Page 17
Answers may vary slightly. Here are some possible answers:
Producers:
  tree
  flowers
  grass
Consumers:
  snake
  rabbit
  deer
Decomposers:
  worm
  snail
  bacteria

Page 18
Synonyms:
  drench, soak
  sprinkle, drizzle
  jump, leap
Antonyms:
  drought, flood
  deep, shallow
  wet, dry
  sink, float
1. b
2. a
3. b
4. b
5. a
6. c

Page 19
Summary C
The written summary must include main ideas, not every detail of your summer vacation.

Page 20
1. $1\frac{1}{4}$
2. $\frac{17}{2}$
3. $4\frac{2}{3}$
4. $\frac{7}{3}$
5. $4\frac{3}{4}$
6. $\frac{19}{4}$

Page 21
2.

3.

4.

5. $\frac{3}{10}$
6. $\frac{8}{10}$ or $\frac{4}{5}$
7. $\frac{7}{100}$
8. .5
9. .6
10. .25

Page 22
2. Southern Hemisphere
3. Western Hemisphere
4. Eastern Hemisphere
5. equator
6. prime meridian
7. North Pole
8. South Pole
9. latitude
10. longitude

Page 23
(top)
Answers to questions may vary. Here are some possible answers:
birds/tree branches
snake/rock
ants/log
duck/water
fish/water
(bottom)
A bird depends on the tree for shelter.
A fish needs water to live in.
A turtle needs water to swim in.
An ant uses a log for shelter.

Page 24
1. import: to bring in from another place
2. audience: a group of people who hear a performance
auditorium: a place for hearing
3. automobile: a machine used to transport someone
automatic: a self-acting machine
4. graphics: relating to writing or drawing
grammar: rules for writing

Page 25
Answers to questions will vary.

b. Shark teeth are interesting and tell us a lot about these great animals.

Page 26
2. 1,410
3. 1,352
4. 144
5. 754
6. 990
7. 3,234
8. 7,304
9. 4,325
10. 5,250
11. 7,684
12. 58,138

Page 27
It was lost in a daze.

Page 28
Answers will vary.

Page 29
2. calcite
3. feldspar
4. igneous
5. sedimentary
6. metamorphic

Page 30
Answers will vary.

Page 31
1. Scott and Steve
2. Scott started the club because he was worried Steve would spend all his time with Henry.
3. Meetings are held in the tree house. You must climb up to the tree house to be in the club. Henry was not able to be in the club because he was afraid of heights. Steve felt guilty about leaving his cousin alone.
4. Steve and Henry
5. Steve started the club because he wanted to do something that Henry could do.
6. Meetings were held on the island. You must swim across the lake to the island to be in the club. Steve couldn't be in the club because he couldn't swim. He understood what it was like to be left out.
7. Steve, Scott, and Henry
8. Scott started the club because he wanted all

three boys to play together.
9. Everyone has fun doing things they can all do together. All three boys played together and had a great summer.
10. quartor, becaus, diffrent, favrite, untill, really

Page 32

a = 4 b = 7 3 + 4 = 7	a = 3 b = 6 3 + 3 = 6	a = 3 b = 9 3 + 3 = 9	a = 5 b = 15 3 + 5 = 15
a = 3 b = 6 3 + 3 = 6	a = 12 b = 15 3 + 12 = 15	a = 10 b = 13 3 + 10 = 13	a = 11 b = 15 3 + 11 = 15
a = 2 b = 1 3 + 2 = 1	a = 8 b = 12 3 + 8 = 12	a = 6 b = 9 3 + 6 = 9	a = 1 b = 4 3 + 1 = 4

2. 1
3. 6
4. 3
5. 10
6. 14
7. 2
8. 13

Page 33
2. 45
3. 16
4. 24
5. 8
6. 11
7. 20
8. 70

Page 34
2. 3:00 PM
3. 9:00 AM
4. 11:00 AM
5. 6:00 PM
6. 7:00 AM
7. 1:00 AM
8. 1:00 AM

Page 35
Static Electricity:
lightning
girl touching can of soda
socks sticking to clothing
hair standing on end
Current Electricity:
television
telephone
light
radio

Page 36
2. ungrateful
3. unhelpful
4. replacement (or misplaced or displacement)
5. disappointed (or disappointment or reappointed)
6. incorrectly (or uncorrected)
7. unwisely

8. disagreement
9. unexpected
10. impolitely

Page 37
Answers will vary.

Page 38
congruent: b, d
symmetrical: a, c

Page 39
2. >
3. <
4. =
6. perpendicular
7. parallel
8. perpendicular

Page 40
2. g
3. d
4. f
5. a
6. b
7. c
8. e

Page 41
2. crust
3. mantle
4. pressure
5. magma
6. lava
7. active
8. dormant

Page 42
1. simile
2. metaphor
3. personification
4. Answers will vary.

Page 43
a) 6
b. 2
c) 7
d) 1
e) 4
f) 9
g) 3
h) 5
i) 10
j) 8

Page 44
2. 30%
3. 20%
4. 10%
5. Friday

6. Wednesday
7. 5
8. Wednesday to Thursday

Page 45

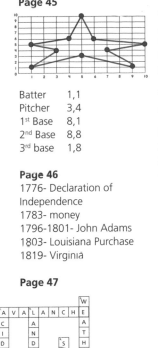

Batter 1,1
Pitcher 3,4
1st Base 8,1
2nd Base 8,8
3rd base 1,8

Page 46
1776- Declaration of Independence
1783- money
1796-1801- John Adams
1803- Louisiana Purchase
1819- Virginia

Page 47

							W			
A	V	A	L	A	N	C	H	E		
C		A					A			
I		N		S			T			
D		D					H			
R		S					E			
A		G	L	A	C	I	E	R		
I		I			L			I		
N		D						N		
		E				G	R	A	V	I	T	Y
						O				
						C				
						K				
						S				

Page 48
2. Setting: hospital
   Mood: serious
3. Setting: Sally's room
   Mood: hopeful
4. Setting: Mrs. Grady's Garden
   Mood: happy

Page 49
1) This summer, my dad wanted to fix up our house. 2) He read an article in "Home Improvement" magazine about how to do repairs. 3) We didn't have many tools at our house. 4) My dad had a saw, a hammer, and some nails. 5) We tried to do the repairs, but my dad's tools were too old. 6) We weren't able to fix anything correctly. 7) So I decided it was time to ask for some help. 8) I looked through the Chicago Gazette for an advertisement. 9) I saw an ad for a man named Mr. Fix It, so I wrote him a letter. 10) I told him to come to 355 Mulberry Street and help us with our repairs.

11) A few days later Mr. Fix It showed up at our house. 12) He knew how to do just about everything. 13) He had all kinds of great tools, so the job was fast and easy. 14) What would we have done without Mr. Fix It ? 15) Within a few days, everything was fixed. 16) The only problem was that my dad's old tools were all broken!

Page 50
2. $3.55
3. $0.15
4. $10.00
5. $8.00
6. $0.40

Page 51
2. 20% = .2
3. 15% = .15
4. 12% = .12
5. 8% = .08
6. 4 kids

Page 52
1. Apache
2. Cherokee
3. Comanche
4. Creek
5. Crow
6. Iriquois
7. Navajo
8. Paiute
9. Shoshone
10. Sioux
11. Ute
12. Cherokee
13. Navajo
14. Sioux
15. Iriquois
16. Apache
17. Creek
18. Comanche
19. Shoshone
20. Ute
21. Paiute
22. Crow

Page 53
2. e
3. c
4. d
5. a

Page 54
2. B
3. B
4. A
5. A
6. B

Page 55
"Oh no!" said Pam. "We'll never be able to sail without some wind."
"We just need to be patient and wait for the

wind," Sam said.
Pam said, "We can't wait around all day. We need to do something."
"What can we do?" Sam asked. "We can't control the wind!"
"Let's close our eyes and think about the wind," Pam said. "Think of the windiest day you can remember."
"Okay," Sam said.
Pam shouted, "Hooray! Now we can go sailing."
The wind even blew Pam's copies of "Sail Away" magazine out of the boat.
"Gee, Sam," Pam said. "You didn't have to think that hard!"

Page 56
-3, -2, -1, 0, $\frac{1}{2}$, .75, 1, 1$\frac{1}{2}$

Page 57
16: 16, ①4, 8, ②
28: 28, ① 14, ②7④
30: 30, ① 15 ② 10 ③⑤6

Page 58
These statements are false:
2, 7, 8, and 9. They are crossed out.

Page 59
2. respiratory
3. nervous
4. digestive
5. immune
6. skeletal
7. muscular
8. lymphatic

Page 60
Conflict: Robin wanted to camp by a lake so she could swim. Katie wanted to camp in the desert where she could rock climb.
Resolution: The family camped at the beach where Robin could swim and Katie could rock climb.

Page 61
2. Inference
3. Fact
4. Inference
5. Fact
6. Fact
7. Inference
8. Inference
9. Fact
10. Inference

Page 62
2. -1 < 3
3. 5 > -5

4. $3 > -7$
5. $-4 < -2$
6. $0 > -3$
7. $-9 < -1$
8. $5 > 0$
   A subzero sandwich.

Page 63
2. -5
3. -6
4. $-3 + -6 = -9$
5. $-4 + -4 = -8$
6. -8
7. -9
8. -9
9. -7
10. -11

Page 64
2. a
3. e
4. c
5. b
6. 4, 3, 1, 2, 5

Page 65
2. photosynthesis
3. sunlight
4. carbon dioxide
5. water
6. chlorophyll
7. oxygen
8. stomata

Page 66
Nouns:
summer
geyser
presidents
drive
Proper Nouns:
Colorado
Reggie
Yellowstone
Mount Rushmore
Verbs:
reached
packed
told
took
Verb Phrases:
should go
will have
could hardly believe
had bought

Page 67
Answers will vary.

Page 68
1. 14
2. 26
3. -2
4. 10
5. 9
6. 1
7. 3
8. 6
9. 3

Page 69
2. feet
3. miles
4. centimeters
5. 16 ounces
6. 200 pounds
7. 30 pounds
8. 2 tons

Page 70
New England:
   Ship building
   Fishing
   Lumber
   Mills
   Wheat
Middle Colonies:
   Wheat
   Mills
   Factories
Southern Colonies:
   Wheat
   Rice
   Tobacco

Page 71

Page 72
2. Baleen
3. plates
4. plankton and krill
5. porpoise
6. killer whale
7. humpback
8. gray

Page 73
2. gerund
3. gerund
4. verb
5. gerund
6. verb
7. gerund
8. gerund

Page 74
2. right
3. isosceles
4. scalene
5. isosceles
7. $a = 40°$
8. $a = 155°$
9. $a = 70°$
10. $a = 60°$

Page 75
2. parallelogram, $C = 135°$
3. trapezoid, $D = 155°$
4. rhombus, $D = 165°$
5. rhombus, $B = 60°$
6. parallelogram, $A = 40°$
7. rectangle, $A = 90°$
8. square, $B = 90°$

Page 76
Answers may vary.

Page 77
2. St. Louis, Nashville
3. Los Angeles, Austin
4. Boise, Orlando
5. Phoenix, Las Vegas

Page 78
Dear Phillip,
   How are things in France? I hope you're having a good summer. My summer has been really fun. First, I went to computer camp at a nearby college. I learned how to type on a keyboard. They also taught us about how computers work. After computer camp, my cousin Dave came to visit. He lives in Baltimore, Maryland. Dave and I like to swim and play basketball.
   In a few days, I'm going on a vacation with my family. We have a cabin in Maine, and we stay there every summer. We always go hiking, fishing, and swimming.
   Write me back soon and tell what you've been doing this summer!
Sincerely,
Kevin

Page 79
1. b
2. c
Answers will vary.

Page 80
2. $\frac{6}{8} = \frac{3}{4}$
3. $\frac{2}{2} = 1$
4. $\frac{6}{5} = 1\frac{1}{5}$
5. $\frac{5}{7}$
6. $\frac{5}{8}$
7. $\frac{6}{12} = \frac{1}{2}$
8. $\frac{10}{11}$
9. $\frac{4}{6} = \frac{2}{3}$
10. $\frac{4}{3} = 1\frac{1}{3}$

Page 81
1. $\frac{2}{6}, \frac{3}{6}$
2. $\frac{4}{6}, \frac{1}{6}$
3. $\frac{9}{15}, \frac{5}{15}$
4. $\frac{8}{8}, \frac{6}{8}$
5. 12
6. 18
7. 20
8. 9

Page 82
2. Lewis and Clark
3. Pike
4. Lewis and Clark
5. Pike / Lewis and Clark
6. Pike
7. Lewis and Clark
8. Pike

Page 83
2. The surface is 6,000 degrees Celsius. The atmosphere is millions of degrees.
3. Dark spots on the sun that are cooler in temperature.
4. A million Earths would fit inside the sun, and 109 Earths would fit across the diameter.
5. It gives us light, heat, warmth, and energy.

Page 84
1. summer
2. You can be outdoors day and night. Warm weather is great for swimming, hiking, and boating. Vacation from school gives you freedom and fun.
3. winter
4. You can have fun indoors and outdoors. You can ski, snowboard, or sled. Festive holidays bring families together.
5. Answers will vary.

Page 85
Answers will vary.

Page 86
1. Perimeter: 22 inches
   Area: 28 inches^2.
2. Perimeter: 17 cm
   Area: 15 cm^2
3. Perimeter: 12 yards
   Area: 9 yards^2
4. Perimeter: 36 feet
   Area: 54 feet^2
5. Perimeter: 28 inches
   Area: 40 inches^2
6. Perimeter: 18 feet
   Area: 14 feet ^{2}

Page 87
1. 576 inches^3
2. 300 inches^3
3. 768 inches^3
4. 24 feet^3

Page 88
Alabama: Montgomery
Alaska: Juneau
Arizona: Phoenix
Arkansas: Little Rock
California: Sacramento
Colorado: Denver
Connecticut: Hartford
Delaware: Dover
Florida: Tallahassee
Georgia: Atlanta
Hawaii: Honolulu
Idaho: Boise
Illinois: Springfield
Indiana: Indianapolis
Iowa: Des Moines
Kansas: Topeka
Kentucky: Frankfort
Louisiana: Baton Rouge
Maine: Augusta
Maryland: Annapolis
Massachusetts: Boston
Michigan: Lansing
Minnesota: St. Paul
Mississippi: Jackson
Missouri: Jefferson City

Page 89
Montana: Helena
Nebraska: Lincoln
Nevada: Carson City
New Hampshire: Concord
New Jersey: Trenton
New Mexico: Santa Fe
New York: Albany
North Carolina: Raleigh
North Dakota: Bismarck
Ohio: Columbus
Oklahoma: Oklahoma City
Oregon: Salem
Pennsylvania: Harrisburg
Rhode Island: Providence
South Carolina: Columbia
South Dakota: Pierre
Tennessee: Nashville
Texas: Austin
Utah: Salt Lake City
Vermont: Montpelier
Virginia: Richmond
Washington: Olympia
West Virginia: Charleston
Wisconsin: Madison
Wyoming: Cheyenne

Page 90
Answers will vary.

Page 91
Answers will vary